BECOMING Tamara

A STORY BY
TAMARA RIVERA

Copyright © 2025 by Tamara Rivera

All rights reserved. No part of this publication may be reproduced, distributed, or transmitted in any form or by any means, including photocopying, recording, or other electronic or mechanical methods, without the prior written permission of the author, except in the case of brief quotations embodied in critical reviews and certain other noncommercial uses permitted by copyright law.

Printed in the United States of America

ISBN 979-8-89114-156-8 (hc)
ISBN 979-8-89114-154-4 (sc)
ISBN 979-8-89114-155-1 (e)

Library of Congress Control Number: 2024926082

2025.03.12

MainSpring Books
5901 W. Century Blvd
Suite 750
Los Angeles, CA, US, 90045

www.mainspringbooks.com

Introduction

Becoming Tamara is more than a story, it is a journey of self-realization, courage, and the unwavering pursuit of authenticity. This book follows the path I walked as a transgender woman, coming to terms with my true self. It explores both the joys and the trials of embracing an identity that I had hidden for so long.

In these pages, you will find moments of doubt, sparks of hope, and the courage it takes to stand firm in the face of misunderstanding and adversity. With every chapter, my intention is to share the essence of what it means to step forward, reclaiming not only my name but my spirit, piece by piece.

This book is for those who have questioned their path, worth, or belonging. I hope this message resonates with those searching for their voice and those supporting others on their journey of becoming. Welcome to a story of reflection, struggle, resilience, and triumph. It's about discovering the power of owning your authenticity.

Contents

Introduction v
A Heartfelt Letter to My Friends and Supporters. ix
A Brief Timeline of Transgender History xi
    Gender Transition. 1
    From Tomas to Tamara. 6
    Life-Altering Decades 9
    The Planning Steps. 12
    Faith Prevailed 17
    Born Again. 25
    Post-Surgery, The Journey Back Home 28
    A Challenging Recovery 32
    I Got This. 39
    The Birthday Queen. 43
    At the DMV. 47
    The LA Festival of Books 52
    Vocal Cord Surgery. 60
    The Woman With Four Birthdates. 68
    The Love Letters. 71
    Social Media Engagement. 73
    The failures of Online Dating. 76
    Recognitions. 80
    Transgender Advocacy 83
    The Gender Affirming Letters 91
About the Author 103

A Heartfelt Letter to My Friends and Supporters.

To my friends and allies, I extend a heartfelt gratitude. I want to share with you my gender transition process. This is a deep personal experience, and an impactful journey, that I am happy to share with you.

With gratitude and vulnerability, I began a new chapter in my life in Miami, Florida on March 5th, 2024. I was there for ten days and returned home to recuperate.

I want to express my heartfelt gratitude to all those who supported me. Your constant support has given me strength, and I am touched by the love, understanding, and compassion you have shown.

This is not only a personal milestone; it represents the triumph of authenticity and self-discovery.

Your support shows the strength of compassion and inclusivity. Your kindness has made a positive impact on my life in a challenging landscape.

I extend my gratitude to those who have stood by me, offering encouragement, understanding, and acceptance. This has made my journey more bearable and given me the strength and courage to embrace my gender identity.

Amid a world filled with uncertainty and hatred, I am fortunate to find happiness and compassion in the company of my caring friends. I cherish every moment spent with you, as our radiant smiles radiate style and glamor.

In conclusion, thank you for being a part of my life and standing by me during this transformative moment. Together, we are breaking down barriers and fostering a world where everyone is free to be their authentic self.

With love,

Tamara Rivera

A Brief Timeline of Transgender History

Throughout ancient times, historical records document transgender people. Cross-gender identities have been identified in various cultures, from the Neolithic and Bronze Age to ancient Greece and other civilizations. Throughout recorded history, transgender individuals have existed, even though the term "transgender" didn't become common until the mid-20th century.

- In 1965, the word transgenderism was coined by psychiatrist John F. Oliven of Columbia University.
- Some historians consider the burial of a male skeleton in women's clothing in feminine grave goods to be an early transgender burial, dating back 4,900 to 4,500 years.
- In 1931, in Berlin, Germany - Dora Richter became the first known transgender woman to undergo vaginoplasty.
- In 1941, Barbara Ann Wilcox, a transgender woman, became one of the first individuals to change her name through a successful court petition in Los Angeles County.
- In 1952, Christine Jorgensen underwent male-to-female sex reassignment surgery, which created a global sensation.
- In 1959, The Cooper Do-nuts Riot occurs at Cooper's Do-nuts in Los Angeles, LAPD arrested rioters. Transgender women, lesbian women, drag queens, and gay men riot, one of the first LGBT uprisings in the U.S.
- In 1965, John Money founded the Johns Hopkins Gender Identity Clinic.
  - Gender identity differs from the assigned gender at birth, which is male or female. For most people, gender identity relates to the designated gender at birth. However, some people experience little or no connection between their sex and gender.

- In the past, the medical community labeled transgender and gender-incongruent individuals as having a mental health disorder called "gender identity disorder." However, this attitude is no longer considered valid.
- In August 1966, Transgender women and Vanguard members led the Compton's Cafeteria Riot in San Francisco's Tenderloin district.
- This incident was one of the first recorded transgender riots in the United States, preceding the famous 1969 Stonewall Riots at the Stonewall Inn in New York City's Greenwich Village.
  - The Stonewall riots were a pivotal moment for the LGBTQ rights movement, both in the U.S. and abroad.
- In 1970, Sylvia Rivera and Marsha P. Johnson founded the Street Transvestite Action Revolutionaries (STAR) in New York City as an activist organization for transgender and gender non-conforming individuals, following the Stonewall uprising.
- In 1980, Steve Endean created the Human Rights Campaign Fund.
- In 1999, Gwendolyn Ann Smith, a trans woman who works as a graphic designer, writer, and activist, created the Transgender Day of Remembrance.
  - The Transgender Day of Remembrance commemorates Rita Hester, who sadly lost her life in Allston, Massachusetts.
- In 1999, Monica Helms, a trans woman and U.S. Navy veteran, designed the transgender pride flag, and first displayed it at the 2000 Phoenix Pride parade.
- In 2008, the murder of Angie Zapata, a transgender woman, occurred in Greeley, Colorado. The court found Allen Andrade guilty of murdering Angie Zapata, who was a transgender woman, and charged him with a hate crime.
- In 2009, Rachel Crandall, a transgender activist from Michigan, established The International Transgender Day of Visibility.
  - It aimed to address the lack of holidays dedicated to transgender people within the LGBT community.

- In 2015, President Barack Obama made history by appointing Raffi Freedman-Gurspan as the first openly transgender employed in the White House in.
- In 2015, Caitlyn Jenner made history as the first openly transgender person featured on the cover of Sports Illustrated.
- In 2019, Palm Springs, California, made history by electing America's first all-LGBT city council. The council included three gay men, a transgender woman, and a bisexual woman.
- In 2023, Parents and Friends of Lesbians and Gays created TNET, its Transgender Network, as an official "Special Affiliate" with equal privileges and responsibilities to its regular chapters.
- In 2023, Ashley Burton, a 37-year-old black transgender woman, was murdered in Atlanta, Georgia. Ashley's death is the ninth violent killing of a transgender or gender non-conforming person, and the second one in Georgia this year.

The Triumph of Transgender Trailblazers

Transgender individuals have overcome challenges and made history by fighting for equal rights with strength and dedication.

At the core of this narrative, there are individuals whose stories resonate with the resilience of the entire community.

Struggle, discrimination, and a relentless fight for acceptance often marked their paths. Yet, through sheer determination and unwavering self-belief, they have emerged as beacons of hope and catalysts for change.

Activists like Marsha P., Johnson, and Sylvia Rivera were pioneers in the LGBTQ+ rights movement. Figures like Laverne Cox and Janet Mock have also made significant contributions to progress and inclusivity by breaking stereotypes and redefining beauty standards.

Their contributions extend beyond activism and advocacy, permeating every aspect of society. Anohni and Juliana Huxtable, both transgender artists, have defied norms and expanded creative expression in the arts.

In politics, Danica Roem and Sarah McBride have broken barriers and spearheaded policies for equality and justice.

In the fields of science and technology, transgender pioneers such as Lynn Conway have made significant contributions, pushing the limits of innovation and discovery.

Their drive and imagination have not only enriched our understanding of the world, but also inspired future generations to dream without limits.

The journey of transgender individuals involves overcoming challenges and promoting diversity. It reminds us that everyone, regardless of gender identity, has an important role in creating a fair and inclusive world.

As we celebrate transgender people and their strength, we recognize the difficulties that still exist.

We commit to creating a society where everyone can be themselves without discrimination or judgment. Our stories show us that resilience can turn hardships into hope and adversity into opportunities.

The Impact of Transgenders on Society

The transgender movement has had a big impact on different aspects of the world, including activism, culture, and careers.

1. **Social and Political Activism:**
   - The Cooper Do-nuts Riot (1959) and the Stonewall Riots (1969) were pivotal moments in LGBTQ+ history, including transgender individuals, as they sparked widespread activism for equal rights and paved the way for the modern LGBTQ+ rights movement.
   - Transgender activists have played crucial roles in advocating for anti-discrimination laws, healthcare access, legal recognition of gender identity, and inclusion in various aspects of society.

2. **Representation in Government:**
   - Transgender individuals have increasingly held positions in government, advocating for policies that promote equality and inclusion.

   For example, Danica Roem became the first openly transgender person to be elected to a U.S. state legislature in 2017.

3. **Contributions to Modern Society:**
   - Arts: Transgender artists and creators have enriched the cultural landscape with their unique perspectives and storytelling. Their work often addresses themes of identity, acceptance, and diversity.
   - Fashion: Transgender models and designers have brought visibility and diversity to the fashion industry, challenging traditional norms and promoting inclusivity.
   - Medical Fields: Transgender healthcare professionals and researchers have contributed to advancements in transgender healthcare, including hormone therapy, surgical techniques, and mental health support tailored to transgender individuals' needs.

4. **Education and Awareness:**
   - The transgender movement has raised awareness about gender diversity and contributed to educational initiatives aimed at fostering understanding, empathy, and acceptance of transgender people in society.

Overall, the transgender movement has visually transformed society, with colorful pride flags waving proudly in the streets during parades. The chants and cheers of supporters fill the air, accompanied by the rhythmic beat of drums and the blaring sound of horns.

The scent of unity and acceptance permeates the atmosphere, creating feel hope and belonging for all individuals, regardless of their gender identity.

Gender Transition

Gender transition surgery is a personal decision. Not every transgender person will choose to undergo the procedure. However, if you are considering gender transition surgery, you might wonder why you should consider it necessary.

Religious believers argue God created you with intention. Should you question or defy the creator? Some allege that God's intention is to punish or condemn you, which mirrors my own experiences before and after I came out as a transgender woman. As a result, I lost friends both offline and online, with some drifting away while others tried to force their religious beliefs on me. They accused me of going against God and committing a grave sin.

The Bible does not forbid changing one's gender; however, there are some people who lack education and understanding about transgender identity. This lack of knowledge can be influenced by factors such as politics, religion, or ignorance. Transition means embracing and expressing the way you look, and matches your gender identity, not your assigned sex at birth. The decision becomes complex when you think about the expense of surgery without insurance, and you must consider the potential complications.

Before undergoing gender transition surgery, you must have consultation with specialists. These specialists include professionals who will evaluate your mental health. This evaluation is important because specialists conduct it before you undergo major surgical changes.

As a digital creator with a large, engaged following, I extend my influence beyond the written page, fostering community and inspiring positivity through my engaging online presence. My passion for fashion, beauty, and creativity also flows into my work, reflecting a vibrant individuality that resonates deeply with my readers and followers. My work is a testament to my resilience, commitment to authenticity, inclusivity, and my unyielding pursuit of a world where everyone feels empowered to be themselves. Maintaining a positive mindset has influenced how I approach my goals and interact with others. Through my travels, I have been fortunate enough to experience various cultures and foster personal growth. Ultimately, the combination of these elements has come together to shape an individual who is deeply committed to personal and societal progress.

The journey of coming out as Tamara was challenging. I was ready, and the timing was perfect. While I could have done it earlier, there were undisclosed life events that needed to be resolved.

Pain shaped my life, but through it all, I remained strong and faithful to my journey. I always dreamed of becoming the woman I felt connected to in my heart. I started by seeking help from a psychiatrist and a therapist while I was going through a host of emotional traumas.

Obstacles came my way when I revealed my gender transition. Losing friends and being rejected by my family made me feel like my world was falling apart. I found a new family in my closest friends that became my strongest allies and influenced who I am today and formed unexpected bonds with others. My friends on my social media accounts are aware of my gender identity and admire and respect me. My transition journey was supported and strengthened by every therapist session. They concluded I had firm determination and that my faith and determination were my greatest strengths.

Through therapy and consultation with specialists, I received the support needed for my transition. To keep myself healthy and mentally prepared, I exercised, lost weight, ate right, slept well, and developed healthy habits. In October 2023, a significant turning point occurred when I chose to medically transition from male to female. After coming out and changing my identity, the next obstacle was undergoing gender transition surgery. I was ready for the challenge, but it ended up being more difficult than I expected.

My gender transition journey lasted over a year, beginning with a consultation with my surgeon. Throughout this process, I conducted extensive research on gender transition, even watching YouTube videos for additional information. As the months led up to September 2021, I took meticulous steps to prepare myself for coming out as a transgender woman.

Amidst the challenges of the COVID-19 pandemic, I purchased women's clothing, shoes, makeup, and various other items while working from home. These actions were an essential part of my transition journey, allowing me to create distance from my previous male persona.

Despite my age, I was strong, healthy, and ready to embark on this momentous step as a transgender woman. As long as I stay faithful to God and myself, I believed my dreams were possible, regardless of age. On March 5th, 2024, my transformative path officially began. As I gazed at my reflection in the mirror, I couldn't help but notice the intricate details of my facial appearance. The contours of my cheekbones, the sharpness of my jawline, and the slight arch of my eyebrows were all features that I held dear to my heart. The decision to forgo face feminization surgery was rooted in my deep connection with these distinct characteristics. I chose not to have the surgery known for enhancing facial features to create a gentler feminine appearance.

Besides using estrogen hormones to make my breasts bigger, the key changes I made to my body were getting hyaluronic butt injections. These injections gave my flat posterior a much-needed lift and added volume. Despite the pain, I am now satisfied with the outcome.

I thought about breast augmentation, but my surgeon convinced me it was unnecessary. He explained my breasts were blossoming and suggested waiting six months for the hormones to take effect before revisiting the topic. It is important to note that breast augmentation can lead to negative outcomes and side effects, such as lumps and other procedure-related issues.

Given the surgeon's honesty and the value I placed on his advice, I trusted his judgment. As a first step, I underwent laser hair removal to eliminate unwanted facial and body hair. Ever since I first grew body and facial hair, I have despised it.

I started shaving my legs at twelve and have since shaved my body hair and underarms occasionally. Laser hair removal made a positive and significant impact, and I feel more confident in my body. I opted out of getting laser hair removal for my legs because my hair is minimal and thin. I only shave occasionally, and I can go months without noticeable hair growth.

I also considered electrolysis for facial hair removal. This was due to my age and the presence of some white hair on my face. Laser hair removal cannot effectively target the white pigment on the hair follicle. However, electrolysis can help remove the remaining facial hair on the face and neck. I cannot stand the discomfort of the needle piercing though the hair follicle, but it is something I had to deal with.

At last, the news that I eagerly expected arrived! As soon as 2024 began, I received approval for gender reassignment surgery with Dr. Whitehead at Restore Medical in Bay Harbor Islands, Florida. On March 2, 2024, I will go to Miami, Florida for the surgery taking place on Tuesday, March 5.

Finally, my lifelong dream of becoming the woman I have always wanted is coming true.

"Hold on to your dreams. It's too soon to give up now,"

— *Tamara Rivera*

From Tomas to Tamara

I carefully searched for a female name that reflects my gender identity and has a historical connection. I wanted a name that would be both beautiful and meaningful. Exploring various historical figures and their stories became an integral part of my decision-making process.

I delved into the lives of influential women who had paved the way and fought against societal norms. Their determination and resilience inspired me, and I sought a name that would honor their legacy. It was crucial for me to find a name that would stand the test of time, resonating with both my personal journey and the collective struggle of countless women throughout history.

During this step in my transition, I had to carefully consider my choice of names. I wanted a name that I could proudly carry with me.

After careful consideration, I settled on the name Tamara. This decision came after months of exhaustive research, as I was looking for a beautiful female name with a historical connection. The name originated from the Biblical name "Tamar," which appears in Genesis 38:21. Interestingly, it holds the meaning of "palm tree" in both Hebrew and Arabic. This name carries a special significance and conveys a strong sense of femininity.

The name later spread to the English-speaking world in the 1930s and gained popularity in the United States in the 1970s, and it also gained popularity during the medieval period in Eastern Europe.

The film called Tammy and the Bachelor contributed to the name's common usage in the United States from the 1950s to the 1990s. Today, Tamara remains popular worldwide for its pleasing sound and historical significance. In my life, I have experienced the painful sting of agony, the piercing sound of insults, and the heavy weight of humiliation caused by individuals who lacked understanding of transgender experiences.

I remember being subjected to derogatory names that seared into my ears, leaving scars of injustice. To make matters worse, people unfairly branded me as gay, a label that struck me like a suffocating odor, tainting my identity.

Coming out is a challenging experience, especially without the support of a loving family. Many transgender individuals can undoubtedly empathize with this struggle. My journey as a transgender woman begun with the important step of seeking guidance and help. While I hope you have a family that embraces and supports you, it is essential to recognize that not everyone is open-minded when it comes to diverse gender identities.

Following a comprehensive evaluation, I was fortunate to be prescribed HRT hormones by an LGBT doctor. I have been working diligently with a therapist and actively taking part in a local support group. These activities have kept me occupied as I strive towards my goal of openly and confidently coming out in both my personal and professional life.

I faced fear head-on and took significant steps towards my goal. Initially, I engaged in a discussion with my manager at work regarding my desire to transition. Subsequently, I proactively composed a letter addressed to the HR department, wherein I articulated my intention to publicly embrace my identity as a transgender woman and undergo a name change. Now, as I embark on a new journey at my employer, I am filled with excitement and gratitude.

It is truly thrilling to work with a company that not only values its employees' health and wellbeing but also embraces diversity wholeheartedly. I am humbled by the countless amazing individuals who have played a part in reaching this milestone.

I want to encourage you as you face life's challenges. Be bold and persistent in confronting them. By doing so, you gain the courage and strength to conquer your fears. Also, remember that there are local resources available to help you.

Keep in mind that you are not alone on this journey. It is crucial to prioritize both your physical and mental well-being, all the while nurturing a positive mindset.

Previously, transitioning to a new gender posed challenges due to the limited resources available prior to the advent of the internet and mobile technology. However, in today's world, the internet has emerged as an invaluable tool for accessing information on transitioning.

It is crucial to exercise caution when perusing online material concerning this subject. Not everyone has the best intentions for your health, growth, and success as you navigate the challenges of coming out. For instance, I have encountered transgender individuals online who seek information from unreliable sources, which can ultimately lead to unforeseen dangers and consequences. Make choices based on what you want, not what others think.

"No path is revealed without a clear vision."

– *Tamara Rivera*

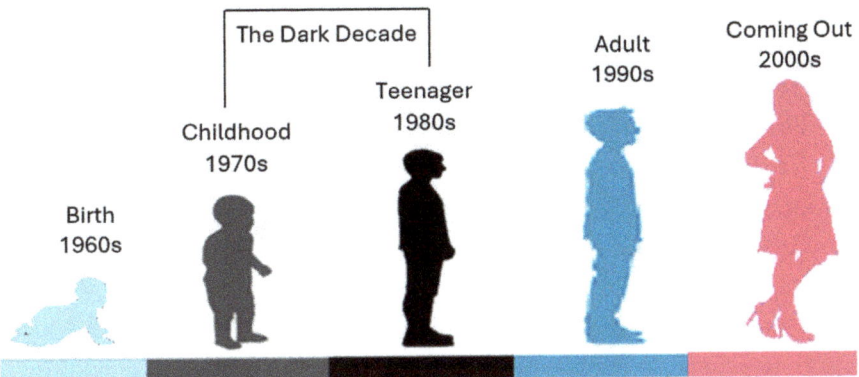

Life-Altering Decades

During the 60s, the exploration of identity defined my childhood. It was at the tender age of five when I embarked on my first journey into gender exploration.

Even now, the memory of that moment remains vivid in my mind. I was filled with curiosity about the absence of breasts on my body. This considerable experience has shaped my life.

For much of my life, I yearned to have natural, feminine curves, feeling as if a vital piece of mine was absent and leaving me incomplete.

During the troubled 70s in Puerto Rico, serious issues like rape, child abuse, gender dysphoria, lack of education, and unemployment were rampant.

At twelve, I endured my initial encounter with sexual assault perpetrated by my uncle. Regrettably, this distressing incident set off a cycle of shame, as more violations took place involving other boys and even my father.

As a result, I faced derogatory comments, being labeled as gay. I never felt that this truly represented my sexual orientation. I was oblivious to alternate gender identities and where I belong within the gender spectrum.

The eighties ushered in an electrifying new phase in my journey. As July 1981 rolled in and I set foot on American soil once again, I had to reacquaint myself with the nuances of the English language. Alongside this, I braced myself for the daunting trials of navigating a relationship with my abusive father.

This experience made me more self-reliant. It also brought back intense emotions related to my gender dysphoria. I had encountered difficulties in dealing with it. I left the comforts and beauty of Puerto Rico and never returned to the land I loved.

The painful memories I left behind, like a dream I didn't want to relive. My life experienced unexpected changes during the 90s. I tied the knot, welcomed two kids, relocated, and found my identity as a transgender woman.

The early 2000s allowed me to express my gender identity. When I embraced my authentic self at 59 and started living as a woman, my marriage ended. However, this marked the beginning of a new chapter in our relationship. I moved out of our house to live with two female roommates for two years, sharing a cozy apartment in the heart of the city. However, because of financial struggles, I decided to move back in with my ex-wife and our two children in our old family home.

Although we now live under the same roof, our lives have taken separate paths, and we occupy different rooms. We're committed to sharing the costs and responsibilities of owning a home. Our goal is to create a harmonious environment for our family.

Throughout the decades, unexpected events have shaped my life, each one leaving an indelible mark on my journey of self-discovery. I have pondered, questioned, and emerged from the depths of introspection, leaving behind the shadows of my past and focus on my personal growth.

Signifying dreams is a mystical phenomenon that surpasses our understanding. They transport us to a realm where vibrant images and captivating melodies intertwine, painting a vivid tapestry in our minds.

As we succumb to the enchantment of our dreams, our senses are immersed in a harmonious symphony of delightful emotions, while our eyes indulge in a vibrant kaleidoscope of colors. Fragrances, delicate and soothing, caress our olfactory senses, immersing us in a world of tranquility.

Yet, now and then, dreams possess an unexpected power. Like a lightning bolt in the stillness of night that startles you awake. Their intensity pierces through the serenity, leaving us shaken, as we grapple to make sense of the message.

> *"Your dreams are the window to your future.*
> *Follow your dreams."*
>
> — *Tamara Rivera*

The Planning Steps

I had 85 days left until my next birthday when I decided to undergo gender transition surgery from male to female. I faced criticism but still I moved forward. I prepared myself for this moment for over a year before the surgery by taking critical steps to change my life. Every therapist I talked to had the same basic questions.
- Have you ever thought of harming yourself or someone else?
- Have you ever thought of killing yourself?

My "no" resonated powerfully, answering both questions. After a month of planning before the surgery, I reserved the hotel room, flight, and a required caregiver to travel with me at least three months before the surgery. Despite enduring child abuse, rape, and a challenging childhood, I have always felt God was there for me. He listened to my cries and provided me with hope for my gender transition.

God was there for me during the toughest times, and I owe my life to him. Even when I questioned my gender and had doubts, he listened in silence. Decades later, the response finally came at the right moment. I planned meticulously and worked on improving myself. After coming out, my focus was on achieving my goal.

I began my transition by losing weight. By September 2021, I was nearly two hundred pounds. In January 2022, I caught sight of myself in the mirror. Despite receiving compliments from friends that I did not need to lose weight, I realized how serious the situation was. I decided to take drastic measures. My mindset did not align with theirs because I could not truly see my weight until I confronted myself in the mirror and accepted that it didn't reflect my true self.

The current situation called for a shift in direction. I bought a digital scale on Amazon and regularly tracked my weight. I woke up every day at 6 am, checked my weight, and exercised daily. During my morning routine, I exercised thirty to forty-five minutes and later went for an hour-long walk at lunchtime. I walked up to five miles outside daily after work.

Over the course of nine months, I increased my daily step count from 2,000 to 20,000+ steps. This significant improvement was driven by my desire to lose weight, and it inspired me to become more committed to my fitness routine. As a result, I experienced a steady weekly weight loss ranging from one to three pounds.

I changed my diet to include lean meats, more veggies, and controlled my hunger to lose weight and get fit. At night, my roommates often made fried chicken. The smell made me hungry, so I ate nuts and drank fruit juices to curb my hunger. I eliminated salt, sugar, and fat from my diet. As a result, I had more energy and better health. I also gained better control over my cholesterol and high blood pressure.

Through my dedication and perseverance, I was able to experience a notable reduction in stress and anxiety, ultimately leading to a series of positive transformations in my life. I felt more joyful and optimistic as a result. Taking the time to prioritize self-care had a profound impact on my daily existence, enhancing its overall quality. It was truly remarkable to witness the positive changes reflected in the mirror as well. I realized that being Tamara empowered me and motivated self-care.

The effects of my efforts resulted in a shrinking waistline. Over the course of nine months since I first began my exercise regimen, I embraced and prioritized my daily routine. I made these changes, not on the advice of a doctor, but because I made a conscious decision to adopt a healthier lifestyle, shed weight, and enhance my physical and mental wellness. The rewards were worth the effort. I lost thirty pounds in nine months. In the wake of that initial success. It took two additional months to reach a weight of one hundred and fifty-five pounds. My weight remained unchanged until surgery.

Although I had a desire to lose five pounds, I was not too concerned because the gender transition surgery would assist me in achieving additional weight loss. I combed through online resources for weeks to find the best surgeon for my gender transition surgery. It soon became clear that none of the doctors in nearby states met my criteria for gender reassignment surgery.

I was aware in advance that the cost was going to be high, and I may have to bear the financial responsibility alone. Insurance was not available in the state of Georgia. During my research, I uncovered the alarming fact that many clinics in my state are engaging in false advertising for gender transition surgery. After making phone calls, I found out that these clinics only offer top surgery, not gender transition surgery.

After discovering the offices of Restore Medical in Miami, I talked with Dr. Whitehead. I was already undergoing laser hair removal with Milan Laser Hair Removal. Despite assurances of coverage, I encountered issues with my insurance.

The insurance requested two therapist letters in order to demonstrate the medical necessity for coverage of laser hair removal. I put in a great deal of effort. I undertook the task of collecting these letters to support my claim and focused on drafting a persuasive letter to bolster my case.

I received a letter from Jamie, my new therapist. However, I was hesitant to start therapy with another therapist for the second letter. The letter was crucial for my laser hair removal approval, which was necessary for my pre-surgery preparation.

The insurance company continued to reject my claim for laser hair removal despite my efforts and appeals. I had no option but to cover the expenses out of pocket. Having a scheduled surgery at Restore Medical on early March 2024, I wanted to avoid any further delays caused by this decision.

My transition unfolded according to plan, even though I rarely dedicated much time to extensive planning. However, this time, I made a point to outline every crucial aspect well in advance. The week before the surgery, everything fell apart. Because of an unforeseen medical emergency, my friend Nina proposed to travel with me, but she called to cancel the trip after months of preparation.

Nina called me on the Sunday, a week before our Southwest Airlines flight, to apologize for not being able to come. Her son had a medical emergency. I was caught off guard by the news. I dropped to the floor crying after I hung up the phone. "What should I do?" I wondered. The flight was in five days and the hotel and airline ticket were nonrefundable.

These events almost made me cancel my plans. However, I required a caretaker to accompany me until March 12, 2024. Just moments before my scheduled flight, my insurance advisor and I found ourselves in a frenzy of phone calls and hectic activities, leading to utter chaos.

I was frantically seeking someone to assist me in my time of need. With each passing day leading up to the flight, my frustration continued to build. Despite the promises made, not all organizations had qualified medical professionals available. There were others that couldn't provide a companion during my stay.

I thought I was losing my sanity, as I couldn't have a phone conversation with anyone. Every call ended in tears of desperation, keeping my insurance advocate busy. She made calls, even off work. I would love to meet her and show my gratitude with a hug for all her help.

The day before the flight, a candidate from Florida, who had potential, offered to help. However, because of her inability to accept insurance, she requested payment in cash. I couldn't afford it because I used $4,000 from my retirement savings and had to pay $3,500 to Restore Medical.

On the day of the flight, I felt an overwhelming sense of solitude as I headed towards the surgery that was scheduled. Despair washed over me and my heart sank as my small glimmer of hope faded mercilessly. Many questions flooded my mind about the obstacles I was facing. While I had the desire to return home, I was overcome with an unwavering belief and trust to continue progressing, undeterred by the obstacles.

When I arrived at the resort, which was ideally situated one block away from the offices of Restore Medical. I encountered a frustrating situation where I had no help available. I had only four days until the scheduled surgery, and the combination of frustration and overwhelm was taking its toll on me. Because the doctor's office policy said I needed someone with me for the surgery. I thought about going home two days early.

I found myself in a situation where I had no one to accompany me, not even my children or family. This lack of support made the experience of being on my own incredibly challenging, often bringing me to tears. It became clear that I couldn't handle everything by myself. In just two days, I would return home, but for the surgery to proceed, I needed someone to take care of me. Thankfully, in my moments of desperation, it was only God who heard my cries and provided me with comfort.

"It's easier to jump over a brick wall than to run into it."

— Tamara Rivera

Faith Prevailed

On a gloomy Sunday morning, March 3rd, just two days before the surgery, I rose tiredly from my bed and savored the aroma of freshly brewed coffee wafting through the air. Feeling a deep sadness, I made my way back to my room from the elevator. Each step I took seemed to carry the burden of my disappointment, weighing me down like a looming dark cloud.

As I sat down for breakfast, the clinking of cutlery against the porcelain plate echoed in the silent room, a stark reminder of the solitude I felt. Tears streamed down my face as I savored every bite of my last meal. With no one by my side, I knew I had to make the tough decision to cancel my reservations.

The sound of my voice quivered as I made the phone calls, each cancellation feeling like a knife piercing through my already shattered emotions. After canceling the hotel reservation and the surgery itself, I realized I had one more task to complete. The realization hit me like a punch in the gut; I needed to reschedule my flight to return home just as I arrived.

The thought of returning home without the expected surgery brought tears to my eyes. As I reached out to grab the phone, a wave of surrealism flooded over me. After all this progress, how did it end like this?

The weight of the situation settled in my chest, making it difficult to breathe. A surge of tearful emotions, a physical reminder of the profound disappointment I felt, accompanied each touch of the phone's buttons, my fingers pounding the dial pad like a hammer hitting a rock.

At that moment, I realized prizing having a caretaker by my side. Their support and help would have been crucial for me to overcome this hurdle and proceed with the surgery. Instead, I had to confront the harsh truth of heartbreak and uncertainty all by myself.

While staying in Florida's Harbor Bay Islands, I had the opportunity to stay at the renowned Grand Beach Resort Hotel. I was lucky enough to have a spacious room that comfortably accommodated up to six adults. As soon as I walked in the room, I was greeted by a cozy atmosphere. The room featured a spacious double sleeper sofa and a coffee table, creating a welcoming space. To the right, there was a small bathroom with a refreshing shower. As I continued to explore the room, I discovered a hallway and a larger spacious bathroom with a shower. The main room was equipped with two queen beds, double closets, a TV, and a balcony just a few steps away.

There is also a hallway and a spacious bathroom with a large shower. In front is a long table with a coffeemaker, cream, sugar, four drawers, and a safe. The main room has two queen beds, double closets, a fifty-inch TV, and a balcony, just a few steps away.

I called the hotel reservation desk to explain my issue. It is possible that my reservation cannot be canceled. I may not be able to get a refund because the fees were pre-paid and non-refundable. The situation intensified, and I felt devastated and financially stressed. I begged the reservations desk to understand that I was here for surgery, not for leisure. Being alone, I couldn't afford to lose my money, and I had to leave.

The sound of a woman's cry has a way of softening people's hearts, I thought to myself as I climbed into bed. At that moment, I couldn't help but feel a sense of loneliness and frustration. As I lay there, immersed in my prayers and tears, a flood of questions overwhelmed me. Why had God led me to this point of humiliation, defeat, and devastation? With tears, I finally accepted the circumstances and laid my head on the pillow.

As I was drifting off to sleep, I received an unexpected call from Elena, a friend I had met in Atlanta just two weeks ago. Despite not expecting her call, she asked how I was doing. With tears in my eyes and a deep, sad voice, I explained to her I was preparing to go home tomorrow morning. Unfortunately, I could not undergo the surgery because I couldn't find anyone to stay with me.

Feeling disheartened and exhausted from my futile attempts at making stressful calls, I finally reached a breaking point. At that moment, I reached out to Southwest Airlines to inquire about the possibility of an earlier flight back home. However, Elena intervened and reminded me of the considerable distance I had traveled and the immense value this journey held for me, considering the hard work and determination I had invested. With a soft whisper she said, "You cannot return home Tamara; I won't allow it, I will be there tomorrow morning." As I lay in my cozy bed, tears streamed down my face, tracing a path of saltwater over my flushed cheeks.

The soft glow of moonlight filtered through the curtains, casting a gentle, ethereal light on the room. Lavender filled the air with a soothing scent. It brought me comfort and I felt at peace. In that moment, I felt an immense joy that made me feel warm and content.

I held the belief that God had indeed answered my prayers. Despite facing immense pain through trials and tears, He stood by and sent an angel to be there for me.

My life has been shaped by countless tears and overwhelming pain, humiliation, and the sense of defeat, but my faith in God remained unwavering. Achieving my goals required enduring hardships, but my unwavering faith and determination lead me to success.

The next morning, I desperately called the hotel's reservation desk to make sure my reservation was still valid. Simultaneously, I contacted the doctor's office to inform them I would be there on schedule for the surgery. I didn't need to call the airline to reschedule my flight. The day of the surgery had finally come, and I was ready.

Two days prior, I was required to complete several essential steps and adequately prepare for the surgical procedure. This included doing the bowel preparation, using antibacterial soap for my shower, brushing my teeth, and making sure I have paid Restore Medical. I also could not eat or drink anything after midnight. It was important to bring the prescribed antibiotics, Bromelain pills, Arnica pills, and compression stockings for the surgery. The list emphasized the importance of compression stockings in preventing complications and warns that failure to bring them could lead to the surgery being canceled.

I began the bowel prep in the morning with the products my doctor prescribed. He gave me a shopping list, saying that without these items, I couldn't have the surgery. By Sunday and Monday, I adhered to a liquid diet, getting ready for the surgery by Tuesday morning.

The scheduled arrival time at the clinic was 8:30 am on March 5th. I arrived 30 minutes early with Elena. We waited for a short time before an office staff member invited us inside. Sitting in the waiting room, time seemed to drag on. The sterile smell of the clinic hung in the air, filling the room. However, after a mere two minutes, Marie, the nurse, appeared before me, her warm smile lighting up the room.

She guided me to a small room where the sharp smell of disinfectant hung heavy. Marie measured my weight and checked my vitals, her gentle touch calming my nerves. As she handed me a hospital gown, the cool fabric brushed against my skin, a stark reminder of the impending surgery. I followed the staff down a long corridor, the sound of footsteps echoing against the sterile white walls. They led me into an examination room, where the crisp white sheets of the bed beckoned me to lie down.

Moments later, a surgeon entered the room, his presence commanding attention. He was a tall, handsome Hispanic male, his confidence shining through his every move. As he approached, smelling antiseptic mingled with his cologne, creating a unique mix of clinical and masculine fragrance. With a calm demeanor, he administered the anesthesia, trending the needle barely registering before my eyes grew heavy and I succumbed to sleep.

Upon waking up, a dim light filled the room from afar. The nurse, standing by my side, provided a comforting presence. As I slowly regained my senses, she helped me get dressed, her gentle touch providing reassurance. As the anesthesia coursed through my veins, a nauseating sensation twisted my stomach into knots, making it churn and roil.

Suddenly, a powerful surge of bile surged upward, escaping my body in a fountain-like eruption. The acrid stench of vomit filled the air, mingling with the sterile aroma of the clinic. Through it all, the reassuring voice of the nurse cut through the chaos, assuring me that this was a normal side effect and that I would soon recover.

She confirmed the surgery was a success. Her words brought me comfort and gratitude. Elena, my caretaker, and the nurse nestled me into a wheelchair, ensuring my comfort with soft pillows on the seat.

As I left the clinic, I was greeted by a gloomy day outside. The sky was adorned with low-hanging clouds, and a gentle drizzle created a soothing pitter-patter sound. Shortly afterwards.

As we made our way through the block, the wheels of the wheelchair rolled over the rough pavement, creating a slight vibration that resonated through my body. The adventure took us through a parking lot, smelling gasoline and concrete filling the air. We ascended a steep hill. The strain in Elena's muscles was clear, but her determination was unwavering.

Finally, we reached the hotel, and the elevator ride up to the sixth floor provided a brief respite from physical exertion. Once settled in my room, the softness of the bed and the warmth of the blankets enveloped me, providing a sense of comfort and security. I knew that the road to recovery would be long, but in that moment, I felt a glimmer of hope and gratitude for the caring individuals who guided me through this post-surgery adventure.

Lying in bed, I had a urine bladder positioned on my right side and a blood drainage container on my left. The meticulous placement of these medical devices was accompanied by precise instructions to my caregiver on draining them at specific intervals.

Elena, with gentle determination, faithfully followed my doctor's instructions, her footsteps softly padded on the floor as she guided me from my bed to the bathroom.

The faint scent of antiseptic lingered in the air, a reminder of the sterile environment she maintained to ensure my safety. Despite my efforts to be independent, her watchful eye and caring touch kept me safe from harm.

She ensured I had my medications and meals on time, and we enjoyed engaging in conversations. She was also an author, and we swapped books.

In the morning, after I woke up, she took care of emptying both bladders and later went down the elevator to get me my breakfast; she knew what I wanted: scrambled eggs with onions, mushrooms and pepper jack cheese and a cup of coffee.

During the four days following the surgery, Elena diligently attended to my needs. I found myself confined to my bed, reliant on her help.

Despite my stubbornness and independent nature, I attempted to move occasionally, only to be scolded to remind me that moving out of bed without supervision could have caused me trouble and at least once I nearly fell. The doctor said that if I move on my own without supervision, I could fall and suffer a heart attack and die.

Elena stayed with me and took care of me for the next five days. She was there for me from Monday through Friday; she had to go home to take care of her father. I am deeply grateful for all the help and support Elena provided, going above and beyond to help me.

I wish the circumstances had been more favorable; I had hoped to provide her with more generous compensation, going beyond the provision of meals and a hotel room.

I found myself trapped in a daunting financial predicament, consumed by the weight of a substantial sum of money I had to spend. The total expenses amounted to an astonishing $4,000.00 for a ten-day hotel stay.

The hotel lobby, adorned with luxurious chandeliers, exuded a subtle scent of freshly polished wood, mingling with the lingering aroma of rich coffee from the nearby café.

The air was filled with the sound of busy footsteps, quiet talks, and sometimes the clinking of glasses from the fancy bar. As I checked in, the soft touch of the smooth marble countertop provided a cool sensation against my fingertips. Besides the hefty hotel bill, I paid $3,000.00 to Restore Medical. The clinic's waiting room was filled with the crisp scent of disinfectant, while the sound of gentle instrumental music played in the background, creating a calming atmosphere.

Trending the cold examination table against my back sent a shiver down my spine. I set aside $500.00 to cover meals and miscellaneous expenses. The aroma of sizzling garlic wafted from the nearby restaurant, mingling with the tantalizing scent of freshly baked bread. The clatter of plates and the lively chatter of diners filled the air, creating a vibrant ambiance.

And lastly $500.00 for transportation to and from my destination. The rumble of engines and the honking of car horns reverberated through the busy streets as I navigated my way to the airport. The soft leather seats of the Lyft car provided a comfortable ride, offering a momentary relief from the bustling city outside.

To compound matters, miscellaneous costs also ensnared me. Ultimately, I was compelled to bear the burden of nearly $8,000.00 directly from my pocket, leaving an indelible mark on my already strained finances.

It was a big financial sacrifice, mostly covered with money I borrowed from my retirement account. Without money saved in my retirement, I would not have been able to afford this.

There were moments when I kneeled to pray, and it felt as if my prayers were unheard. The silence would deafen me, leaving me with a sense of despair. It felt like driving through dense fog, unable to see the path ahead. I had felt this way for most of my life, wondering if my pleas were merely echoing in an empty void.

But then, after enduring what felt like an eternity of suffering, a shift occurred. I felt like the heavens opened and my prayers were finally answered. The weight on my shoulders lifted, and a ray of hope pierced through the darkness.

> *"Fall seven times and stand up eight."*
> — *Japanese Proverb*

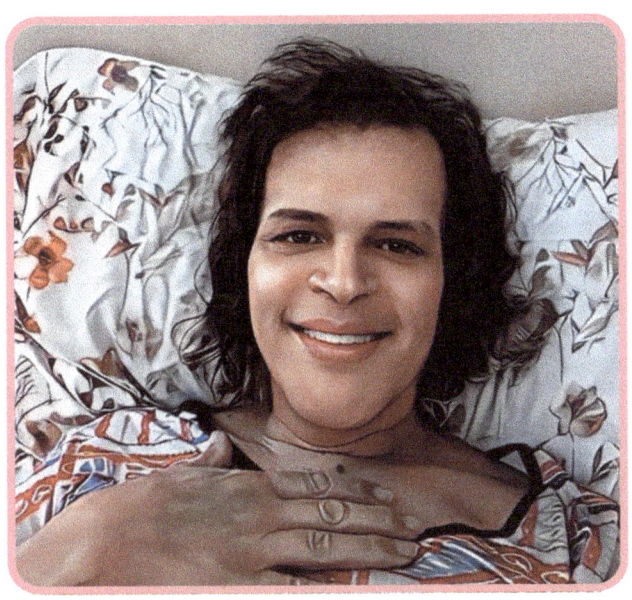

Born Again

My sister Maggie, who lives just five hours away from the Bay Harbor Islands in Florida, offered to come and stay with me for the remaining days from Saturday, March 9th through Tuesday, March 12th.

When my sister finally arrived early Saturday morning in her new black Nissan Murano, we enjoyed a few leisurely days before leaving the resort. I felt a surge of newfound strength coursing through my body. Despite the lingering sluggishness, my movements were becoming more fluid and confident. My appetite returned, and I relished every morsel that passed my lips.

On that delightful Sunday, two days prior to being discharged from the clinic, I mustered enough energy to accompany my sister downstairs to the pool. As we ventured outside, the warm rays of the sun enveloped me, bathing my skin in a comforting embrace. The sight of the shimmering pool beckoned, and my sister indulged in a brief dip while I settled nearby. I savored the tranquility of the moment, basking in the gentle breeze that rustled the leaves overhead. The distant laughter and splashing sounds from the pool created a soothing symphony, lulling me into a state of relaxation.

It was a brief respite before returning to the confines of my room, but it filled me with gratitude for the progress I had made on my journey to recovery. My sister took excellent care of me constantly encouraging me and gave the confidence I needed to venture outside of my comfort zone and explore beyond the boundaries of my room. She went outside of the hotel a few times to buy things I needed and meals at a local Spanish restaurant. We both wanted the taste of the local Spanish cuisine.

Since there were no Puerto Rican restaurants, we opted for Cuban food because of the similarities in the Caribbean cuisine. It's costly there because of the many resorts and exclusive restaurants contribute to the high cost of living in that area. We found some small shops and upscale malls like the Bay Harbor Shops. Their expensive price tag was obvious from the exterior. The sleek black glass and marble building had a gated parking garage with valet service.

I went downstairs one more time with my sister. We enjoyed a good thirty minutes by the pool. Later, I went for a ride in her new luxurious SUV, with a supple leather interior.

As her vehicle's fuel gauge blinked on empty, I enthusiastically asked if I could join her for the ride. After being confined to the hotel for days on end, the prospect of venturing out thrilled me.

I yearned for the chance to savor the journey before returning to the familiar confines of the hotel. With less than a day remaining until the removal of my bandages, anticipation tingled in the air.

The day of the revelation, I was like a child waiting for a birthday to open her presents. I was ready for the bandages to be removed. I woke up early as usual and my sister and I went downstairs for breakfast one last time before leaving the lovely Grand Beach Resort Hotel at Harbor Bay Islands.

After enjoying a delicious breakfast, we headed up to the sixth floor using the elevator. Our main goal was to gather our bags and complete the check-out process. As we made our way up, I couldn't help but reflect on the unforgettable memories experienced at the Harbor Bay Islands Resort. It was a memory that would stay with me forever.

"The journey may be long and arduous, but the end is rewarding."

— *Tamara Rivera*

Post-Surgery, The Journey Back Home

My sister Maggie and I went to Restore Medical. Dr. Whithead was waiting for me and made a powerful impression. Despite my stubbornness causing him a little stress, he was still nice.

I was there to have the bandages removed, resembling the discomfort of wearing an adult-sized diaper with attached drain tubes and bladders. I walked into the exam room where the doctor performed the surgery. It only took him five minutes to remove the bandages. He examined the healing process, took a photo, and offered to show me the results.

The initial task involved the careful removal of the bandages. With a swift snip on both sides, he carefully grasped the bandages and gently extracted the drain tubes. Although there was some slight discomfort, it was not painful. He then stitched up the incisions caused by the drain tubes and cleaned the wounds. Before concluding, he captured a photograph. I was curious and he asked if I wanted to see the picture, to which I obliged. As he displayed the image, I was not shocked. My gaze scrutinized the depiction, noting the absence of a penis and instead highlighting a vagina. It was as if it had perpetually existed, concealed from my perception. Realizing my authentic identity needed help to be revealed. I have forever embodied womanhood, but now it feels tangible, and genuine. This is the essence of who I have always been.

After getting dressed, Dr. Whithead gave me a warm hug and a heartfelt smile before I left. His smile remains imprinted in my memory, marking the moment I felt completely accepted as a woman. He was genuinely happy for me, and the staff at Restore Medical shared my joy.

Their efforts in restoring me have deeply impacted my life, bringing me a sense of wholeness that I will forever be grateful for. I walked out of the medical center, grateful to God for fulfilling my childhood dream of becoming the woman I aspired to be. After leaving the offices of Restore Medical, my sister Maggie kindly offered to drive me to Miami International Airport.

When I arrived at the airport, I went straight to the terminal for Southwest Airlines. Inside, I asked the staff for a wheelchair to help me. I was provided with a wheelchair, and an airline employee pushed me to the terminal. I had plenty of time after arriving early for my flight. The staff ensures that wheelchair-bound passengers get seated near the gate for early boarding.

There was an elderly couple in wheelchairs. I started talking to the woman next to me. People are drawn to my friendly approach, and I am outgoing and attract the right people with my smile. Tamara boosted my confidence and improved my social skills. While engaged in conversation with the couple, I focused my attention on the woman in her sixties, who possessed a stunning, richly hued complexion reminiscent of warm cocoa.

The bustling city of Atlanta served as her beloved home, while her husband lived in the vibrant metropolis of Chicago, rendering their relationship delightfully unconventional. Respectfully, I refrained from prying into the intricacies of their bond, recognizing that their happiness was paramount. As our discussion unfolded, spanning well over an hour, a genuine connection blossom between myself and the woman.

With every exchange, her curiosity about my origins and future aspirations grew, igniting a desire within me to divulge more about my own journey. I shared I'm a transgender woman who had surgery in Miami. She was surprised because I didn't look like someone who identified as male before. Those words, like a vibrant tapestry, painted a vivid portrait of my identity as a woman. They resonated within me, filling the air with the sweet melody of joy as I navigate my path towards home.

Each syllable, like a gentle caress, transformed me into a changed woman, altering the way the world perceives me. As I pulled a book from my bag, I mentioned I was an author. I politely inquired about her name and dedicated the book to her. Additionally, I shared my email address with her. Although she remained silent, I could tell that I had left a lasting impression on the woman in the wheelchair.

Following the surgery on March 5th, I struggled to move around comfortably, even for short distances within my home. In the first weeks of my return home, members of my church and friends came to visit me. We chatted while I had a meal and casual conversation.

I focused on myself, getting stronger each day. I struggled to move between my bedroom and the kitchen. If I moved too much, my bottom would swell and make it difficult for me to move around. Despite not wanting to, I spent a lot of time in bed. Since I work from home, I exercise in the morning. I add movement to my work routine by dancing, walking, or running in place.

I was accustomed to being active and never felt tired at the end of my workday. Sitting around made me more tired than exercising. I had plenty of energy and as long as I kept moving; I was content with my routine. I no longer struggle with anxiety and depression. My daily routine involves waking up and going to bed at the same time, eating consistently unless with friends, and valuing consistency.

"Success isn't always about greatness. It's about consistency."
— Dwayne Johnson

A Challenging Recovery

I used to spend my weekends immersing myself in the vibrant colors of blooming flowers. Additionally, I would revel in the lively chatter of bustling crowds in malls and the alluring scents of captivating places. To capture the essence of these moments, I would take selfies and record videos. It was a joy to share these experiences with my followers on social media.

With my unique fashion sense captivating their attention, I proudly displayed it in my posts. However, now my focus has shifted towards healing and gradually getting back to my daily routine. A primary concern that arises with extended bed rest is gaining weight. Despite my persistent efforts to shed weight and achieve physical fitness, this worry remains constant.

In the upcoming months, I will have restricted movement, and I will be confined within the walls of my home. Here, I carefully balance between the tranquility of sleep and the ardor of writing. Within this space, I achieved the monumental task of completing my second book, and now, I am engaged in the writing of my third book, delving into the profound story of my transition from male to female. This chapter of my journey proved arduous, filled with uncertainties about the recovery process. While I cannot confirm any complications, unexpected challenges emerged, adding a touch of unpredictability to my path.

At the Gynecologist

On April 2nd for the first time in my life and after the surgery I visited a gynecologist. The surgery this far has been free of complications aside from the swelling in the pelvic area, which has been of great concern since it has been nearly a month and when I swell up, it becomes an inconvenience to move around.

I had an appointment at 8:30 at WellStar Women's Health. Despite knowing that I shouldn't be driving, especially a car with a manual transmission, I arrived twenty minutes early. However, it was the only car I had, and since I was home alone, I didn't have any other options. The first step at the gynecologist's office was to provide a copy of my driver's license and insurance card. Since my insurance only provides a digital card, they asked me to send a copy by email, which I had to submit twice because the first one failed.

I felt a sense of unease as I cautiously maneuvered through the cramped space, my movements restricted by the lingering effects of the surgery. The room felt suffocating, as the air was heavy with the smell of antiseptic. Each step was a struggle, my once nimble body now hindered by the aftermath of the procedure. I shuffled back and forth to the front desk, the sound of my footsteps echoing in the sterile environment. After what felt like an eternity, a call came through ten minutes past my scheduled appointment.

With weary legs, I entered the consultation room and gingerly positioned myself on the cold examination bed. Exhaustion washed over me; my energy depleted from the mere act of walking from the car to the clinic. The surgery, still fresh in my memory, made any movement a laborious task.

The young woman, new to transgender patients, began with the customary health inquiries directed towards cisgender women. Patiently, I explained my reason for being there, following up on my gender reassignment surgery. However, her confusion remained clear, and it became apparent that this was her first encounter with someone like me.

Despite her persistent questioning, I maintained my composure, politely responding to each of her inquiries. As she summoned the doctor into the room, it became clear that he hailed from a Middle Eastern background. His rich, dark complexion and the authenticity of his accent left no room for doubt.

When I informed him about my recent gender reassignment surgery, his suggestion was for me to go to the emergency room at the hospital, where a surgeon with appropriate equipment can conduct a more comprehensive examination and perform additional tests, he was unable to help me but gave me advice.

I left the Women's Health center and went to the ER at the hospital a quarter of a mile from where I was. Upon reaching WellStar Hospital at Cobb, on Austell Road, I proceeded to the Emergency Room. Despite my efforts, I couldn't find an available parking space on the upper deck in front of the ER, as all spaces were occupied.

I consider myself fortunate to have been able to secure a parking spot on the lower level, which is conveniently close to the steps to the upper level. I was relieved from having to go through the hardship of a lengthy walk. The architects cleverly designed the steps with shallow risers, allowing for a smooth and effortless climb.

Making my way up to the front door of the ER, I took my time and walked at a slow pace. Upon my arrival, a line was forming at the check-in desk. Even with just five people in front of me, I couldn't endure the idea of standing in line. I addressed the officer stationed at the security desk, located right next to the bustling check-in counter, with respect. With a calm tone, I informed them I would be patiently waiting my turn, taking a seat nearby.

I explained that due to my inability to stand for long periods, it would be more comfortable for me to remain seated. I sat near the check-in desk and patiently waited for the five individuals ahead of me to complete their check-in process. Once it was my turn, I stood up and approached the desk. A middle-aged woman sat there, and I kindly explained to her my physical limitations, emphasizing that I had recently undergone surgery and couldn't stand for extended periods of time.

She gently assisted me into the sleek, metallic wheelchair, the smooth surface cool against my skin. With a kind smile, she began asking me the routine questions before skillfully maneuvering me through the bustling hospital corridors. The faint scent of antiseptic lingered in the air as we made our way to the designated area for wheelchair patients.

As I entered the busy ER waiting room, a symphony of voices and beeping machines filled the space. The harsh fluorescent lights overhead cast a sterile glow, illuminating the worried faces of other patients. I settled into the wheelchair, surrounded by the constant hum of activity.

Throughout the long day that stretched before me, the doctors conducted various tests, each one accompanied by a distinct sensation. The prick of a needle drawing blood, the warmth of a urine sample cup in my hand, the gentle pressure of a swab against my skin.

The doctors and nurses moved around me with focused precision, their footsteps echoing on the tiled floor. Despite the uncertainty and discomfort, I found solace in conversation. Engaging with the compassionate nurses, I shared snippets of my life, my voice filling the air. Their genuine interest and warm smiles lifted my spirits as I basked in the attention that surrounded me.

Amid everything going on, I revealed my identity as an author, sparking excitement among the nurses. Though I had no physical books with me, the vibrant images on my phone and the QR code I created became a portal to my literary world. The technology fascinated them, and they scanned the code, ready to explore my book on Amazon.

With time passing, the final tests awaited me. The whir of the CT scan machine filled the room as I lay still, the cool surface of the table beneath me. The flash of the camera captured images of the surgery area documenting my journey. Some nurses, unfamiliar with transgender patients, embraced the opportunity to expand their knowledge, their curiosity shining through. In this hectic environment, amidst the sounds, smells, and emotions, I found a sense of camaraderie.

The hospital became a temporary home for the five hours I was there, and the nurses became allies on my path to healing. At the end of all the tests and examinations, they came back with the results and told me that the only problem they found was a urinary tract infection.

They gave me an antibiotics injection and a prescription for five days and sent me home. I took the antibiotics as prescribed for five days and I took time to relax and enjoy my time off. Or did I? I was following my surgeons' instructions, but I had other commitments. It was difficult for me to stay in one place. Dr. Whitehead told me after the surgery that it will take three months for me to fully recover. Until then, I should avoid sexual intercourse and exercise.

- On April 2nd, I visited a gynecologist and the ER at Cobb General where I spent all day for a urine tract infection.
- Twenty-seven days after the surgery on April 9th, I went to the Georgia Department of Motor Vehicles to change the gender on my driver's license from male to female.
- I remained at rest for the next ten days and on April 19th I was on a flight to the LA Times Festival of Books and returned home on Tuesday morning at 2:00 am.
- After my arrival back at my home on April 24, a surge of confidence coursed through me, urging me to explore the bustling city center. Excitement filled the air as I strolled through the vibrant gardens, adorned with a kaleidoscope of blooming flowers.

- On April 30th I went to a food festival, the aroma of sizzling delicacies from the local festival of international cuisine enticed my taste buds. The lively sounds of laughter, music, and chatter enveloped me, creating a symphony of joy.
- On May 2nd, I noticed the uncomfortable swelling in my pelvic area, enduring for an eternal three days. The sensation was far from pleasant, leaving me in a state of constant unease.
- My primary care doctor prescribed me steroid tablets to ease the swelling and reduce inflammation.

Most of my time at home was spent immersed in writing, the rhythmic clacking of the keyboard filling the air. Smelling the comforting aroma of freshly brewed coffee, keeping me focused and energized. As the words flowed effortlessly from my mind to the page, I lost track of time. But not everything needs to be spoken aloud. Some secrets are better left hidden, adding an air of intrigue and mystery to my writing. I reveled in the power of the unsaid, knowing that it held a special allure for the reader.

Amidst my busy schedule, organizing for my upcoming 62nd birthday in May brought comfort. Today, on May 13th, 2024, I marked the passing of time, realizing that I had 15 days left before my eagerly expected Zoom interview with Logan Crawford. Each day fueled my creativity as anticipation grew. I knew that this interview held the potential to unlock new doors, to share my thoughts and ideas with a wider audience.

But before the birthday celebrations and the interview, I had a prior commitment. In just two short days, my 62nd birthday will arrive, a milestone to be celebrated with friends near and far.

As I navigated the intricacies of my schedule, I couldn't help but feel a sense of purpose and excitement. Each day, I got closer to the milestones that lay ahead, and I relished the knowledge that my journey was filled with both mystery and purpose. Today May 20, 2024, I felt strong enough and better able to move around, slowly but steadily I am amazed by my quick recovery. I have no discomfort, and the steroids I took for five days helped with the swelling on my pelvis. Although I still cannot walk at my usual pace, I was able to walk with little discomfort or swelling, which made me realize it was time to get active.

"Exercise is the foundation to a healthier body and a positive mindset. Get off the couch and get physical."

— *Tamara Rivera*

I Got This

With my newfound strength and energized spirit, I went for a walk at the Silver Comet Trail. Eagerly embracing this surge of determination, I set off on a long-awaited journey, breaking free from the confines of my home. Despite spending a significant amount of time on social media and writing, I also find relaxation in reading, watching movies, or simply enjoying the cool breeze on my porch.

    Today, however, held a special significance. I felt a renewed sense of happiness as I started my journey on the picturesque walking path near Atlanta, Georgia. As I stepped outside, the warm rays of the sun caressed my skin, bathing me in its golden glow. The temperature soared to a delightful 77°, and the skies above were an unblemished canvas of vibrant blue. Donning a vibrant ensemble of pink, from my visor cap to my shirt, shorts, and tennis shoes, I felt a surge of energy course through me. Equipped with a refreshing bottle of water, I hopped into my car and drove a mere mile to reach the nearest access point of the trail, conveniently near my home.

My trusty selfie stick is a must-have whenever I step outside. It serves as my reliable companion in capturing and sharing my thrilling escapades with the world. I love exploring unknown places, capturing beautiful landscapes with my camera, and cherishing those memories forever. The vibrant hues, intricate textures, and breathtaking panoramas that I encounter awaken my senses. Reverberating through the air, the gentle click of my camera shutter expertly encapsulates the essence of the moment.

The refreshing scent of nature envelops the surroundings, infusing the atmosphere with a revitalizing fragrance. As I embark on my expeditions, the thrill of anticipation courses through my veins, heightening my excitement. I enjoy freezing moments with photos, documenting my journey with videos, and live streaming my experiences on social media to share with others. I capture up to fifty or more vibrant pictures, ensuring that I capture every intricate detail of my experiences. I carefully sift through each photograph, selecting the visually captivating images worthy of preserving.

Occasionally, amidst the hustle and bustle of life, I stumble upon moments that capture pure comedy. With a click of my camera, the scene comes alive, filled with vibrant colors and playful imagery. The sound of laughter echoes through the air as I immortalize these comical snapshots. With a grin, I eagerly share these gems, spreading joy to my loyal followers.

I left home at 3:15 pm, the warm afternoon sun casting long shadows on the deserted trail. As I stepped onto the path, a gentle breeze whispered through the trees, rustling the leaves and creating a soothing soundtrack.

The air carried the faint scent of pine, blending seamlessly with the earthy aroma of the forest floor. With each step, I could feel the softness of the moss beneath my feet, offering a cushioned embrace. Without a set destination in mind. I embarked on my leisurely journey, immersing myself in the tranquil solitude of nature. As I strolled along, I found myself pleasantly distracted, completely losing my sense of time and distance. The captivating sights that unfolded before me beckoned me to capture their beauty through the lens of my camera. The vibrant colors, the gentle rustle of leaves, the sweet aroma of blooming flowers, and the exhilarating sensation of being immersed in nature's embrace enthralled me.

As I approached the elegant stone bridge, its solid structure stretched gracefully beneath the busy road. The hum of traffic above created a soothing sound, adding to the ambiance. Pausing for a moment to soak in the essence of my journey, I recorded a video, capturing the vibrant sights and melodic sounds that enveloped me. As I glanced at my Fitbit, I felt amazed to discover that I had already taken 3,250 steps. What truly astounded me, however, was the overwhelming sensation of comfort and renewal that embraced me, as if weariness and unease were foreign entities in this serene setting.

I went back and kept track of my journey. While walking to my car, I saw a mysterious concrete tunnel with a stone face. I was curious, so I investigated. I have visited this place before, and I noticed it has undergone some renovations. As I look to the left, I was greeted by the sight of a fully equipped open-air gym, and to the right of the gym a skating rink. Sunlight streams in, creating a warm and inviting atmosphere.

Moving ahead, I hear the faint sound of wheels gliding smoothly on the surface of the skateboard rink. The rhythmic noise adds to the vibrant energy of the place. The rink is divided into sections for both children and adults, ensuring that there is plenty of room for everyone to skate freely. The vast area appeals to all ages, inviting feelings of exhilaration and freedom. I snapped a few more pictures, and when I finally returned home from my walk, I glanced at my Fitbit. It was 5:00 pm, and I was astonished to see that I had taken 7,665 steps - the most I had walked since my surgery. I was happy and felt accomplished, no; I exceeded my goal. I am looking forward to going further and I hope to do at least 10,000 steps before I go to Florida to visit my surgeon one more time to be released from his care.

I feel excited about getting better and being able to move freely on my own. I was no longer depended on walls or a wheelchair to move around and I felt liberated. Every small step I take is rewarding and helps me become stronger. Despite my progress, I cannot shake off my lingering worries. A searing pain shoots through my body, intensifying with every slight movement. It is a piercing sensation that commands my attention, reminding me of the recent surgery.

The sensation is akin to feeling my flesh tearing apart, as if the delicate threads of my healing process are being strained. It reminds me that this was no ordinary procedure; it was a major surgery that demands careful attention and respect. Major surgery is a profound procedure, characterized by the meticulous opening of a significant body cavity, the extraction of an organ, or the intricate repair of a substantial body part.

This intricate process may also entail the intricate dissection or transection of tissues, with each incision accompanied by the distinct sounds of surgical instruments. The sterile environment fills with smelling antiseptic solutions, while the surgeon's skilled hands create a sense of reassurance and fragility through their touch. As the operation unfolds, time stretches, as if the body's healing process demands utmost patience.

> *"Healing after surgery is a journey of patience, resilience, and self-care, every step a testament to your strength."*
>
> *— Tamara Rivera*

The Birthday Queen

I thoroughly enjoy organizing important occasions well in advance. To ensure my friends could mark their calendars, I sent out invitations a month prior to my 62nd birthday celebration.

On the evening of May 30th, as the moonlight danced upon my birthday, I felt an undeniable, regal aura enveloping me. I adorned myself with golden strap stiletto shoes that shimmered with every step.

My bodycon dress, crafted in a radiant shade of gold, clung to my curves with confidence. A banner emblazoned with the words "Birthday Queen," draped elegantly across my chest, proclaiming my royal status.

Completing my ensemble, a gold crown rested upon my head, accentuating my commanding presence.

I had gathered a select few loyal friends to celebrate alongside me, I arrived at the restaurant early. A delightful symphony of anticipation greeted me. The air buzzed with animated conversations and laughter, creating a harmonious blend of excitement and joy. As I took in the scene, the aroma of delectable cuisine wafted through the air, tantalizing my senses and heightening my anticipation.

Some friends arrived early. Their smiles and embraces made me happy. I waited for the arrival of my complete entourage, knowing that the fullness of the celebration would be worth the brief delay. As I reflected on the significance of this day, a surge of gratitude and happiness washed over me. This year held special meaning, as it marked the first time I could celebrate my birthday as a female, wholeheartedly embracing my gender identity.

The aroma of sizzling meats and freshly prepared sushi filled my senses, adding to the vibrant ambiance. Right on time at 7:00 pm, the rest of my guests arrived, their laughter and excitement filling the air. As we stood outside the restaurant, I could feel the cool breeze gently brushing against my skin, a pleasant contrast to the warmth radiating from within. The soft glow of the restaurant's lights illuminated the surroundings, casting a golden hue on the pavement.

Before we entered, I was greeted with warm wishes for my birthday and compliments on my stunning outfit. The vibrant colors of my dress and the delicate shimmer of my accessories caught everyone's attention, fulfilling my desire for admiration. With confidence, I led my guests inside, the clicking of our heels echoing through the entrance.

The event unfolded at a newly constructed Volcano Steak and Sushi restaurant, radiating an authentic atmosphere with its towering black oriental doors. Stepping inside, I immediately found myself in a world adorned with stunning Korean decorations. The air hummed with the lively buzz of people relishing sushi and gathering around the hibachi tables.

A wave of exotic aromas enveloped us, transporting us to a faraway land. The tantalizing scent of sizzling meats and fragrant spices mingled in the air, teasing our senses and promising an unforgettable dining experience. The interior of the restaurant was a sight to behold, adorned with intricate decorations and traditional Korean artwork. The walls were painted in rich hues of red and gold, symbolizing prosperity and happiness.

The sound of sizzling pans and buzzing sound of conversations filled the space, creating a lively atmosphere. The clinking of glasses and the occasional burst of laughter added to the joyous ambiance. Despite the activity, the restaurant felt cozy and hidden, like a gem in Seoul.

This moment, the culmination of my journey, was a testament to my unwavering determination. Through moments of uncertainty and self-doubt, I had grasped onto my dreams, praying fervently for their realization.

And now, as I stood there surrounded by friends, I couldn't help but marvel at the incredible journey that led me to this point. Interestingly, a recent survey revealed that a staggering 89.4% of people truly enjoy celebrating their birthdays.

It is a time of pure joy and celebration for many, a chance to reflect on the blessings and accomplishments of another year. For those who celebrate for a week or more, the festivities extend well beyond a single day.

After embracing my gender identity as Tamara, I have eagerly expected and thoroughly enjoyed each birthday celebration. The preparation begins well in advance, at least a month beforehand, as I carefully plan every detail. The anticipation continues to grow as I create posts on social media to excite my fans and receive heartfelt birthday wishes.

But why do I eagerly celebrate my birthday? It is because this day holds a special significance for me. It is a day dedicated to acknowledging and celebrating all that I have achieved throughout the year, a personal holiday of sorts. I've put a lot of effort into promoting and honoring the transgender community, and I wanted to remind you of that.

As I blew out the candles on my birthday cake and basked in the love and support surrounding me, I couldn't help but feel a profound sense of fulfillment. This day was not only mine but also for others who've shared a similar journey. The celebration showcased resilience, authenticity, and an unwavering belief in the transformation of dreams into reality.

Success is the product of determination.

— *Tamara Rivera*

At the DMV

After undergoing my gender affirming surgery, I was eager to proudly display my new identity to the world. To accomplish this, I needed a gender affirming letter from my surgeon. This letter would allow me to change the gender listed on my legal documents and driver's license. So, before leaving Restore Medical on March 12, 2024, I obtained the required letter that would enable me to change my gender on my Georgia driver's license. After dedicating 27 days to recovering from surgery, I felt a surge of excitement on April 9th as I realized my strength had returned.

With a swift and confident stride, I maneuvered my Hyundai Veloster, which was equipped with a smooth six-speed manual transmission. Despite my initial worries about using both pedals with my legs, I had no difficulties operating the vehicle. Filled with determination, I eagerly headed towards the driver's license center to change the gender marker on my driver's license. As of 2023, transgender individuals may change their gender on their driver's license in all 50 states.

Inclusivity efforts have led some states to broaden gender options, such as offering a gender-neutral "X" option for non-binary individuals. However, changing your gender on your driver's license can present challenges. Some states require a birth certificate amendment and/or proof of gender-affirming surgery.

As I entered the Georgia DMV License Testing Center early, hoping for a line-free experience, I was disappointed to see about, twenty people waiting in a line that stretched out before me. The sound of hushed conversations filled the air, mingling with the occasional beep of a scanner or printer. Regrettably, due to my recent surgery, I realized standing in line for an extended period was simply not an option for me. I desperately needed a place to sit. Determined to find a solution, I tried my luck and switch chairs along the line, carefully navigating through the bustling crowd. However, as time passed, my discomfort and fatigue increased, making it even more challenging to find a suitable spot.

Just as I was losing hope, a glimmer of optimism emerged when I turned to the young woman standing behind me. I mustered the courage to ask if she would hold my place in line while I took a much-needed break. In doing so, I explained my situation, emphasizing the difficulties I faced in enduring prolonged periods of standing.

Finally, I spotted a chair near the reception desk that was available and quickly positioned myself towards the front, feeling relieved to find a place to rest. When my turn finally arrived, the young woman behind me kindly gestured for me to proceed. As I approached the receptionist, the subtle scent of paper and ink permeated the air, creating an atmosphere of bureaucracy.

I handed her my gender-affirming letter, feeling a mix of nervousness and anticipation in the pit of my stomach. After taking her time to examine the letter and scanning the words with her eyes, she handed me a form that needed to be completed. Politely instructing me to return it to her, I quickly filled out the form and handed it back. Following her instructions, she then directed me to a computer on her left, where I took a number and settled in to wait. Fortunately, the wait wasn't too long before it was finally my turn at window C.

As I approached the agents behind the large counter and glass partition, I was greeted by a young girl with a radiant smile and beautiful dark skin. Her friendly demeanor immediately made me feel comfortable as I handed her the letter, explaining my gender transition surgery and the necessity of updating my driver's license. While I spoke, her captivating dark brown eyes, shimmering like melted chocolate, met mine. Filled with warmth and understanding, her gaze seemed to wrap around me like a comforting blanket. It was then that a beautiful smile graced her face, and I couldn't help but feel a surge of joy.

In response to my words, she congratulated me on my journey, her voice carrying a melodic tone that resonated in my ears. The sound of her words was like a soothing melody, bringing a sense of validation and encouragement.

The change in my driver's license required her to get approval from a manager. As she made the call, I could hear the distant chatter of voices in the background, blending with the faint sound of ringing phones and muffled conversations. The gentle hum of the air conditioning filled the room, creating a calm ambiance. After what felt like an eternity, she called me back, her voice tinged with excitement. Instructing me to face the camera, I obeyed and heard a slight click as the picture was taken. The room was filled with anticipation, adding a touch of excitement to the air as I awaited my new driver's license.

Ten days later, my new driver's license arrived in a small envelope, signaling the start of a new chapter in my life. The crisp plastic and fresh ink served as a reminder of the journey that had been a long time coming. With a mix of nerves and excitement filling my being, I was flying to California to promote my first book. The thought of sharing my story with others brought a surge of adrenaline, causing my heart to race and my palms to grow moist. As I inhaled the scent of airplane fuel and listened to the sounds of bustling passengers, the anticipation in the air only intensified.

As I held my new driver's license in my hands for the first time, I realized that it truly represented me as a female. It was a symbol of the progress I had achieved and the inner strength I discovered. The initial five weeks of my recovery were nothing short of remarkable. Each passing day brought me closer to my goals, with every step forward becoming a new milestone. Slowly but surely, I could feel my strength returning, accompanied by a tingling sensation coursing through my muscles as I pushed myself to keep moving forward.

I met my determination to move forward with even greater strides of improvement, fueled by a surge of energy that propelled me forward. However, the fear of falling while climbing or descending the steps between floors at my home was a constant presence, instilling a sense of caution in every movement. Initially, I approached each step with great care, tightly gripping the railing as I carefully navigated the stairs. As I reached the next landing, a wave of relief washed over me, marking a small victory in my journey towards full recovery.

The walk between my bedroom and bathroom was short, but the longest distance I had to cover felt like the trek to the kitchen to get my meals. The aroma of leftover food or the smell of meals given by friends or church members filled the air, instantly making my mouth water and my stomach growl in anticipation. With each passing day, as my mobility improved, I gained the ability to prepare breakfast and a cup of coffee. The sound of the Keurig coffee machine brewing became a symphony to my ears. As I took that first sip, a wave of accomplishment washed over me, and I savored the taste of the warm, comforting liquid.

Exploring my home became an adventure, as each week brought new discoveries and a renewed sense of independence. With every step I took, I could feel the strength within me grow, serving as a reminder that I was a relentless force to be reckoned with. Choosing to embark on this journey was the most crucial decision in my life. Yet, as I evaluate the progress I've made, I am convinced that it was worth each and every step.

> *"Adventure is the courage to discover new roads along the journey."*
>
> — *Tamara Rivera*

The LA Festival of Books

In 2024, a world of new opportunities as an author unfolded before me. The pages of my first book came to life, its significance unfolding with each word. After pouring my heart and soul into crafting "Tamara's Journey Through Trials and Tears," a memoir chronicling my tumultuous upbringing as an abused child and navigating the discovery of my true gender identity, I finally saw it become a tangible reality on January 5, 2024. As fate would have it, the renowned LA Times Festival of Books was in the works at the prestigious University of Southern California.

During this exciting time, MainSpring Books extended me an invitation to join the festival, which I eagerly accepted. The anticipation was palpable as I eagerly invested in the festival months before my scheduled surgery. I left no stone unturned in my pursuit of a successful book signing and interview. The air was charged with anticipation as I paid for my participation and tirelessly prepared and promoted my presence at the event. The intoxicating scent of fresh ink and the gentle rustling of pages being turned filled my mind as I vividly visualized the momentous occasion that awaited me.

Collaborating with the talented design team since early March, they worked diligently to create an impressive presentation. Every aspect was meticulously prepared and sent to me for approval. The attention to detail astounded me, and I wholeheartedly embraced the work they were doing. The last three sets of graphics were nothing short of beautiful, but I had one minor objection.

In my poignant memoir, "Tamara's Journey Through Trials and Tears," I delve deep into the struggles of my abusive childhood. The narrative vividly captures the highs and lows of my personal journey, evoking a myriad of emotions within the reader. However, there was one aspect that I objected to: the vivid image of a delicate butterfly gracefully emerging from its chrysalis, its wings unfurling with a gentle flutter. Despite my love for butterflies, the sight was breathtaking and made it all the more captivating.

However, the cover of my book showcased a different marvel of nature, a dragonfly delicately perched on a glistening water surface. The contrasting species and their unique developmental journeys fascinated me.

Filled with excitement, I eagerly emailed the design team a compilation of awe-inspiring dragonfly photos and videos. The next morning, my anticipation was rewarded when they shared a mesmerizing image with me. It was a snapshot capturing a dragonfly's transformation in midair, and it left me in awe. I could almost hear the delicate rustle of its wings as they extended gracefully, forming its majestic adult form. The image had such a profound effect on me, evoking powerful emotions and leaving me completely captivated.

In the fifth week of my recovery from gender affirming surgery, I had originally planned to travel to Los Angeles, California on April 18th. However, despite my efforts to secure a room near the LA Times Festival of Books at USC, I had to settle for a different location. Unfortunately, a week before the event, I discovered that my airline reservation was missing from the Southwest app. Panic crept in as I realized my mistake of forgetting to book the flight after making the motel reservation. Feeling determined to rectify the situation, I urgently contacted the airline, hoping for a quick solution.

As I booked a reservation, tears streamed down my face, a testament to how easily moved I am. Despite my pleas, the airline informed me that there were no flights available on the 18th. They did, however, offer me a standby flight, which I politely declined. I had to reschedule my Atlanta to LA flight for the following day. However, there is good news! I secured a flight for the 19th, perfectly aligning with the festival dates on April 20th and 21st.

The Southwest flight 29NQ50 was an arduous and lengthy experience, taking a toll on my body. The seats lacked any cushioning or ergonomic support for comfort, making it feel like a torturous flight straight out of the Twilight Zone. However, amidst this challenging journey, I had an unexpected encounter with a transgender man while traveling to Los Angeles.

Engaging in conversation, the bustling sights and sounds of the airport couldn't go unnoticed. The air was filled with the delightful aroma of coffee and freshly baked goods, adding to the vibrant atmosphere. With excitement, I mentioned my upcoming book signing and interview event at the Los Angeles Festival of Books. Intrigued, he leaned in, his eyes filled with genuine interest. Sharing the content of my memoir, which focused on the difficulties of an abused child's journey to gender identity, I could feel a sense of connection forming between us.

During the flight, we continued our conversation. The hum of the plane's engines and the occasional announcement from the captain provided a backdrop to our discussion. He opened about his own experiences as a transgender man, sharing the challenges and triumphs he had faced along his journey.

As we reached Dallas Fort Worth International Airport, he bid me farewell and disembarked, leaving me with a sense of gratitude for our brief but meaningful interaction. The flight continued to Los Angeles International, carrying me closer to the excitement and anticipation of the upcoming book signing event.

During the second leg of the flight, my attention was completely captivated by my Google Pixel 2 watch. Its rose gold custom case, adorned with a crown of sparkling crystals, shimmered and caught the light. The watch beautifully matched my Google Pixel 8 phone, which seamlessly synchronized with it. Unfortunately, since my phone was in airplane mode, it didn't update to the correct time zone.

As the boarding process for new passengers began, I remained seated amidst the other travelers. Amidst the hustle and bustle, a young man approached me with enthusiasm, expressing his desire to be my seatmate. Intrigued by his eagerness, I happily welcomed his company, feeling a surge of delight at the possibility of sharing the journey with a youthful and attractive companion.

Prior to the flight departure, we started a delightful conversation, and I enjoyed his company. He was a talented comedian who had me bursting with laughter with his hilarious antics. However, things took a turn when the flight attendant asked us to swap seats with a mother and her autistic child. Reluctantly, the young man moved behind me, and I sat between an elderly couple across the aisle to my right. To my surprise, the seating arrangement seemed strange the towering six-foot bulky man sat beside the window, while his wife sat in the aisle seat, leaving me squished uncomfortably in between. The absence of any communication between them only intensified the tense atmosphere. As if that wasn't enough, the man beside me sprawled out, invading my space, and coughed incessantly, filling the air with a discomforting sound. Annoyed and restless, I constantly checked the time, my mind still fixated on the Eastern time zone.

Regrettably, my watch offered no help, which caused me to believe the flight had been two hours longer. As each minute passed, the agony in my tailbone intensified, making the four-hour flight feel like an endless torment. Adding to the complexity of the situation. To my left sat an elderly woman with her right leg in a cast, clearly in discomfort as her face contorted with pain. Despite her obvious suffering, she remained silent, tightly clenching her lips.

As I shifted in my seat, she glanced at me with concern in her eyes. Sensing my unease, she mustered the strength to check in on me. Her voice was gentle and filled with empathy as she asked about my recent surgery. She felt remorseful when I explained the discomfort caused by the cramped seats, her apology barely audible.

To ease the pain, I resorted to standing up every few minutes during the seemingly never-ending flight. However, the airline attendant, with a concerned expression, advised me against continuing to stand in the narrow aisle. Despite the constant throbbing pain and my worries about my post-surgery condition, the journey felt like an eternity. By the time the flight arrived at our destination, I was utterly exhausted. It was already late in the day, around 3:00 PM Pacific time, when I sought help from an airport staff member. With a kind smile, she offered me a wheelchair and guided me towards the shuttle that would take me to the rideshare lot.

The bustling sounds of the airport filled the air, blending with the muffled announcements over the intercom. As we made our way through the airport, I caught faint whiffs of coffee and the distinct scent of disinfectant. The Lyft ride to the Solo Motel on 4760 S Broadway St. was a stark contrast to the luxury of the resort in Harbor Bay Islands, Florida. Unlike the pristine and upscale resort, the Solo Motel had a worn exterior with faded paint and a flickering neon sign. The air was filled with the smell of exhaust from passing cars, and the distant hum of traffic served as a constant background noise. It was truly a far cry from the serene atmosphere I had enjoyed at the Florida Bay Islands resort.

As I arrived at the motel at 4:30 PM, my initial excitement quickly faded. The unfortunate location confronted me with a disheartening sight. While driving through South Broadway Street, I couldn't help but feel a shiver down my spine as I saw makeshift shelters housing homeless people on the sidewalk. The unsettling atmosphere of the surrounding area added to my unease, with an air of fear and vulnerability lingering in the air. It became apparent upon check-in that there were no nearby services or restaurants. In order to grab a bite to eat, I had to walk about a block away. Being in an unfamiliar city thousands of miles away from home and dressed beautifully as a woman for the first time, only heightened my sense of unease and vulnerability.

As I entered the room, I was immediately struck by its impeccable cleanliness. The plush queen size bed seemed to beckon me to relax, while a small desk with a 40-inch TV promised entertainment. Nearby, a convenient small refrigerator stood ready to store refreshments. A private shower awaited, providing a retreat for relaxation. However, what truly captivated me were the opulent, floor-to-ceiling yellow curtains adorning the windows. Their weighty fabric exuded grandeur and cast a warm, inviting glow when the sunlight filtered through. These honey-hued curtains enveloped the room in a cozy ambiance that I cherished. To ensure my privacy and shield myself from prying eyes, I always made it a habit to keep them tightly closed.

However, my initial contentment diminished when I discovered the TV was not functioning. The room felt empty without sound and flickering images. The next day, I reported the issue, hoping for a quick resolution. Despite the staff's attempts to fix it, the TV remained silent, leaving them no choice but to call a repair technician. In the meantime, I found solace in my phone, which granted me access to entertainment through platforms like YouTube, Amazon, and Netflix. I deliberately chose not to use the hotel's network, as safeguarding my privacy and personal data was of utmost importance to me.

On that first night, the fear of someone sneaking into the open motel courtyard and aggressively breaking into rooms kept me wide awake and filled with concerns for my safety. Their footsteps echoed ominously, intensifying my anxiety. I could hear my heartbeat thumping loudly in my ears as I lay there, tense and alert. Exhaustion eventually overcame me, and I rapidly fell into a deep sleep after the tiring flight.

The next day, as the sun peeked through the curtains, I woke up feeling refreshed. The soft rays of light illuminated the room, casting a warm golden glow. I had reserved my Lyft ride to the fair the day before, so I felt well-prepared for the exciting day ahead. The LA Times Festival of Books, a vibrant celebration of literature, was about to begin, and I couldn't contain my excitement. Without hesitation, I quickly got up from the comfortable bed, feeling the soft carpet beneath my feet providing a gentle sensation. Making my way to the bathroom, I turned on the shower and felt the warm water cascade over my body, washing away any remnants of sleep. Although the morning in California was cooler than expected, I got dressed and attentively selected a long, flowing dress in a kaleidoscope of colors. The fabric was silky soft, and the vibrant hues made me smile.

I slipped into a pair of orange low-heel shoes, their soft suede material hugging my feet snugly. The slight click-clack sound they made as I walked added a touch of elegance to my steps. To complement my ensemble, I reached for a black matching shoulder bag, its smooth leather strap resting firmly on my shoulder.

I had planned to wear a black, cold-shoulder dress, but the sudden chill surprised me, and I changed to the long colorful dress I wore on day one of the book fair. As I shivered slightly while stepping out of my room, the cool breeze brushed against my skin. Fortunately, luck was on my side as I stumbled upon a charming Spanish pastry shop just a block away from the motel. The delicious aroma of freshly baked pastries wafted through the air, instantly enticing me to indulge. With warm butter and cinnamon filling my nostrils, I entered the shop, immediately greeted by an assortment of delectable treats filling the display case. Each one grew more tempting than the last. Unable to resist, I treated myself to a flaky pastry and a steaming cup of rich coffee, savoring every bite and sip.

Feeling content and energized, I made my way back to my room, a warm breeze brushing against my skin, the anticipation building within me. Moments later, my Lyft driver arrived promptly at 8:00 am, the sound of the engine humming softly. I hopped into the car, sinking into the smooth leather seats that embraced me, their scent filling the air as we embarked on a short journey to the University of Southern California. The excitement was palpable in the air, mingling with the scent of freshly cut grass and blooming flowers. Just seven minutes later, I arrived at my destination, ready to immerse myself in the literary wonders of the book fair. The bustling sounds of conversations and laughter filled the atmosphere, accompanied by the occasional chirping of birds. As I walked through the festival grounds, the vibrant colors of MainSpring Books' booth caught my eye, their vivid hues shimmering in the sunlight, beckoning me closer.

The organizers, their smiles shining, greeted me with open arms, their warmth embracing me like a long-lost friend. A symphony of scents filled the air, as they presented me with a breathtaking bouquet of fragrant roses, their velvety petals brushing against my fingertips. Overwhelmed with gratitude, tears of joy welled in my eyes, painting the world with a shimmering haze. The first day of the event danced with excitement. Though I tried to remain seated and rest as much as possible, the pulsating energy made it impossible to sit still. A harmonious chorus of authors gathered at the MainSprings booth, taking turns signing books and engaging in interviews.

As the day progressed, the atmosphere grew warmer, mirroring the rising temperature. While my fellow authors sat at the table, their pens gliding across the pages of their books, I found myself nestled in a row of chairs behind them. The camaraderie amongst us, a blend of new and seasoned authors, created an intoxicating aura of inspiration.

After a quick visit to the restroom, I felt the anticipation for my book signing and interview with the Spotlight Network heighten. It was as if time had stretched, allowing me to savor the excitement coursing through my veins. Finally, the long-awaited moment had arrived. With a mixture of nerves and exhilaration, I prepared myself to sign my stack of 40 books. Surprisingly, within just two hours, the ink effortlessly flowed as I etched my name onto each page. As I completed this task, a sense of accomplishment washed over me, leaving me both elated and amazed at what I had achieved.

"Your past does not define you. It's a steppingstone to your journey of self-discovery."

— Tamara Rivera

Vocal Cord Surgery

The process of vocal cord surgery took a few months of planning. Once again, I needed the usual supporting letters from my therapist. Fortunately, reaching out to my former therapist was the easy part. She agreed to write the letter for me. During this time, I persistently practiced my female voice for over three years. Initially, I received speech therapy from Prismatic Speech, but ultimately had to discontinue due to the exorbitant cost.

In the days leading up to the surgery, I dedicated myself to practicing my singing skills. Immersing myself in the melodies and lyrics of my favorite female artists, I passionately sang along to their songs. With only two days remaining before the operation, I checked my vocal pitch using Voice Tools from DevExtras. As I opened the app, a vibrant interface greeted me, promising a comprehensive analysis of my voice.

I anxiously awaited the results, knowing that this would be my last assessment before the surgery. Finally, the numbers appeared on the screen, revealing my vocal pitch. The app showed I had achieved a score of 280.1 Hz, with a range that was 66% female and 1% male. Comparing this to the average range of 165 to 255 Hz for adult women, I felt a sense of pride and accomplishment. Singing significantly helped me in my journey to sound more feminine. However, despite my self-assurance, I still struggled to express myself clearly.

I had difficulty articulating my thoughts due to my rough voice. So, I underwent voice feminization surgery to achieve a softer, higher pitch voice. I yearned for a voice that would exude confidence and femininity, allowing me to communicate with ease. Weeks of planning and discussions with my insurance provider at Aetna led me to reach out to the speech therapist at Emory Healthcare of Atlanta. I wanted to explore the possibility of gender-affirming vocal cord surgery.

As the surgery approached, excitement and anticipation filled my heart. I couldn't wait to hear the transformation in my voice and experience the melodic tones and softness I had always desired. Singing had been my ally, and now, with the surgery, I knew I would finally have the voice I had always dreamed of. I confided in my friend Catherine, and during our heartfelt conversation, she assured me she would be there for me.

Her unwavering support brought me comfort and joy. On the day of the surgery, August 20, 2024, at 3:30 pm, Catherine accompanied me to the hospital. As she drove, my nerves intensified, but Catherine's soothing voice encouraged me to calm down. Her presence by my side was a source of strength. Upon arriving at the hospital, Catherine suggested I inform the hospital staff that she was my sister, allowing her to be involved in my care and be present in the recovery room. In that moment, our bond transcended friendship. We became sisters through the circumstances that brought us together. It was a sisterhood created by God, and tears of acceptance flowed down my face. I embraced Catherine, grateful for her unwavering support.

Those words led to an unexpected discovery, forging an unbreakable bond between sisters. It all began with a radiant smile exchanged at Ulta Beauty, the air filled with the alure of cosmetics and perfumes. As I slowly regained consciousness in the post-surgery haze, Catherine greeted me with a smile and comforting words. She assured me she was there and would not leave, providing a balm to my soul. I realized I had chosen the right person to be by my side through this journey of self-discovery and transformation.

Throughout my recovery, I diligently chronicled my journey, sharing every step on my social media platforms. This allowed me to captivate a rapidly growing audience, who were eager to follow along. On August 20, 2024, I underwent vocal cord surgery, which meant I needed to rest my voice for a week. Now, the moment to speak has finally arrived.

The following was a poll to my friends:

Hello, my friends, my recent vocal cord surgery procedure on Tuesday August 20 required me to rest my vocal cords for seven days, it is time to say a word. I'm just wondering what my first words will be. Perhaps "I want my momma." Just kidding!

- If you were asked to remain silent for seven days, would you do with the time?
- What would you do with seven days of silence?
- What would be your first words after you break silence?
- I know that whatever I say will be something to inspire others.

Amongst all the positive comments the post received this was the best response from one of my long-term followers.

From your friend, June.

That's a very interesting question. I talk to myself so badly, that would be the first habit I would need to break to be able to stay silent seven days. I admit it would be a challenge for me. And knowing me, I would say something like, hello testing. Testing… Definitely keep us posted on what your words are. I'm thinking of you.

After undergoing gender reassignment surgery, I successfully recovered within six months. However, the journey was not without its difficulties. The surgery brought about the challenge of silence. Coping with the inability to speak was undoubtedly tough, and my recovery was further complicated by a ten-day battle with a persistent cold.

The aftercare instructions for managing complete voice rest were:
- Keep pen and paper nearby for easy communication.
- Use a whiteboard or a text to speech app on your phone.

Important to do:
- Stay hydrated by drinking eight to ten glasses of water per day. Avoid caffeine, alcohol, menthol-type cough drops and alcohol-based mouthwash.
- Breath in steam several times a day. You can use the steam from your shower, facial steamers, humidifiers, or trap the steam generated by a hot bowl of water by tenting a towel over your head.
- Change your outgoing voice mail to redirect your callers to text or email.
- Plan activities that do not require your voice.
- Notify people in your environment of your condition.

Avoid the following:
- Throat clearing. Sip water and swallow hard instead.
- Strenuous activity for a week.
- No smoking and no secondary smoke.

Most of these steps were easy to follow, specifically since I don't smoke or drink alcohol. However, I struggled for the next ten days to suppress my cough and throat clearing due to the stress I was under. I was concerned that coughing would cause major damage to my fragile vocal cords. Despite the challenges, I shed tears of relief after my vocal cord surgery and have no regrets - it was my long-awaited wish.

Throughout this journey, I am grateful to my sister Catherine, who supported me every step of the way. Some days, I worried about potential damage to my vocal cords from coughing, while on other days, I felt the stress in my vocal cords as if they were on the verge of breaking apart. Catherine's soft voice, like that of an angel, reassured and soothed me, reminding me of why I wanted this and assuring me I would be okay. As my follow-up appointment with my surgeon quickly approaches on Wednesday, September 4th, I can feel my voice slowly improving. On Labor Day, I woke up around 4:30 am and noticed that the coughing had stopped, and my voice was clearing.

I checked my voice in the morning, like I had been doing for the past few days. As I nestled back into bed, I was overwhelmed with a profound sense of joy. Tears filled my eyes as I experienced the sweet sound of my voice, resonating clearly in the morning air. Gone was the mere whisper that usually escaped my lips; instead, a vibrant "good morning" effortlessly flowed from my mouth. It was a truly heartwarming experience.

Heading back to bed, I craved two more hours of sleep, desperately clinging to my sister's comforting words, "you'll 'be alright." As the sun peeked through the curtains, I reluctantly opened my eyes. Determined to regain my voice, I gingerly grasped a straw and blew into it, the sound barely audible. Frustration welled up inside me as I attempted to hum, but my vocal cords remained silent. Tears cascaded down my cheeks, mixing with the bitter taste of disappointment.

The recovery from my vocal cord surgery ended up taking longer than I initially expected. It took five weeks before I was able to engage in a proper conversation once more. Some days, I found myself only able to whisper out of frustration. After undergoing vocal cord surgery, I found myself having to position my mouth close to the speaker while describing my situation during phone calls. Each time I made a call, it became difficult to effectively convey my message. Thankfully, there were kind individuals who displayed patience and took the time to repeat what they had heard, ensuring clarity and understanding. The sound of their voices resonated through the speaker, while the sight of their lips moving in sync with their words reassured me. The frustration I felt was accompanied by the faint smell of anxiety lingering in the air. Despite these challenges, their efforts provided me with a glimmer of hope during this difficult time.

I encountered communication difficulties when dealing with others, such as a woman at a bustling doctor's office. Amidst the cacophony of ringing phones and hushed conversations, she persistently urged me to speak with clarity or volume. Frustration gripped me tightly as I fought back tears while attempting to convey my message. However, it appeared she lacked any interest in truly understanding me. In utter exasperation, I abruptly ended the call.

During another phone call, I recall conversing with a woman to whom I shared the details of my recuperation from vocal cord surgery. In a gentle tone, she responded, "Take your time, sweety I'm here for you." Her kindness and patience were clear as we shared a few laughs together. Despite my difficulties in expressing myself and her occasional misunderstandings, she listened attentively, making our conversation a delightful experience.

As time passed, the gentle murmur of my voice would slowly return, like a soft melody echoing through the air. It was a delicate dance, a tentative resurgence, accompanied by the faint scent of hope. But just as the words regained their strength, they would fade away, like whispers carried away by the wind.

Frustration nestled deep within my chest, a constant companion. Yet, I knew that healing required the virtue of patience, like a steady hand guiding me towards recovery. Going out with my sister was a lifeline for me. I relied on her to speak on my behalf at times, while struggling to whisper my own words at others. Then, on September 30, six weeks after surgery, I woke up with a surge of anticipation. As I opened my mouth to speak, I could practically taste the excitement in the air.

I closed my eyes and uttered my first clear words, feeling an overwhelming sense of gratitude. A symphony of sounds filled the room as my voice projected confidently for the first time in what felt like an eternity. In that moment, I offered a prayer of thanks to God, grateful for the gift of my restored voice. I reached a 252.2Hz with a 90% female and 0% male score on the voice pitch analyzer, abandoning the use of a synthetic female voice. On Wednesday, October 9, I had my final appointment with my vocal cord surgeon, and it turned out to be a successful revelation of my newfound voice. As I entered the room, the distinct scent of antiseptic greeted my nostrils. The doctor arrived and prepared to test my vocal cords. He sprayed a solution in my nostrils, causing a slight tingling sensation.

I braced myself as he inserted a probe through my right nostril, the gel on its tip providing a cold, slippery feeling. The discomfort was undeniable, but I patiently endured trending being prodded with the medical device. The doctor recorded sounds vibrating my vocal cords, the process creating a faint buzzing sound in the room. To my surprise, as I sat there, the results mirrored those I had recorded at home and the doctor assured me that my recovery is going well.

While shopping at Walmart, the bright fluorescent lights illuminating the aisles. The sound of chatter and the faint hum of the air conditioning filled the store. My heart raced with anticipation as I prepared to test my voice pitch. Using my phone, I recorded my journey, capturing the sights and sounds for my Tik-Tok fans. Walking confidently, I felt a sense of pride knowing that my high frequency now measured at 280Hz, confirming the progress I had made. I could finally say with certainty that my voice was 100% female.

As I continued recording with a big smile and a seance of accomplishment, I suddenly sneezed, causing a momentary pause in my stride. To my left, a gentleman walked down the opposite aisle, his footsteps echoing softly on the polished floor.

He heard me sneeze and without hesitation, he offered a kind blessing, saying, "God bless you." Grateful for his words, I sincerely thanked him. It was the first time I had spoken publicly since my voice had changed, and I was overwhelmed with emotion. Tears welled up in my eyes as his next words reached my ears. He told me that I sounded like his mother.

Humbled and moved by his comparison, I felt an immense sense of validation. I continued walking through the store, speaking to the camera, more people took notice of me. Their kind words filled the air, like a soothing melody. One person complimented me on my sweet voice, while others glanced at me with approval, acknowledging my soft tone.

Amidst the unexpected moments and daily struggles, I realized that life had been good for me. Every tearful moment had only strengthened me, shaping me into a better woman than I was just a year ago. In that store, surrounded by the bustling activity while I recorded my journey. I felt a sense of wisdom and readiness for whatever tomorrow may bring. Age had not defined me, but rather, the experiences had molded me into someone wiser and better equipped to embrace the future. I'm satisfied with the results, although using an app isn't a professional assessment. I am pleased with my desired feminine voice. The vocal cord surgery boosted my confidence in my feminine voice.

> *"Despite what others say, you are not too old to walk through the eye of the needle, you are just getting started"*
>
> *– Tamara Rivera*

The Woman With Four Birthdates

Regardless of the month or time, your birthday is celebrated on the day you were born. However, the accuracy of official birth records can be compromised for individuals born at home under the care of a midwife. In such cases, the recorded birth may not align with the person's true date of birth, resulting in an inaccurate representation of their age. For instance, my first official birthdate is May 30th.

Now, let's turn our attention to significant life changes, specifically a legal name change and a gender transition. Speaking from my own experience, I went through both a name change and a gender change. If you were faced with similar life-altering circumstances, what would you do?

December 30th holds a special significance. It marked my second birthday, the day I legally changed my name from Tomas to Tamara. This name had been associated with pain and child abuse, burdening my life and leaving lasting trauma. This crucial moment not only altered my name but also symbolized my journey towards becoming the strong and confident woman I am today.

It is important to highlight the impact of my gender transition surgery on March 5th, what I consider my third birthdate. This surgery marked a profound new beginning in my life. As I approached the operating table on that momentous day, determination coursed through my veins, signaling the end of my identity as a man. The bright overhead lights pierced through my closed eyelids, casting an intense glare. The rhythmic beeping of the heart monitor resonated in my ears, blending with the distant hum of the medical tools.

The air carried a sterile scent of disinfectant, mingling with a faint metallic tang that heightened the anticipation. As the anesthesia gently coursed through my veins, its coolness enveloped me, lulling me into a state of surrender. Realizing my childhood dreams had materialized.

Subsequently, on August 20, this marked my fourth birthdate. On the day of my vocal cord surgery, the sterile hospital room buzzed with the sound of medical equipment humming and the faint scent of antiseptic filled the air. The surgeon's steady hands moved with precision; their movements accompanied by the rhythmic beeping of monitors. After the surgery, the road to recovery was a long and arduous journey. The sound of my voice, once deep and masculine, now carried a higher, more melodic tone, like a delicate songbird. The sensation of speaking with my newly transformed voice sent a surge of joy throughout my body, like a warm embrace. Finally, I realized that this vocal transition was more than just a physical change - it was a vital step towards embracing my true, feminine identity.

> *"Celebrate every milestone as a journey."*
>
> — *Tamara Rivera*

Seeking a connection

Hello there! I am a vibrant transgender woman who believes in living life to the fullest. My friends often describe me as a fun-loving and positive soul, and I am on a journey to find someone special who I can share the joy of life with.

I have a passion for dancing that is deeply rooted in my Latin heart and soul. Whether it is a night out in the town or an impromptu dance party at home, I am always up for a good beat and great company.

Fitness is a big part of my life, and I enjoy staying active. It is a perfect way to balance out my love for fine dining. I appreciate the art of a delicious meal and exploring new culinary experiences. Let's share a plate of our favorite dishes!

I'm not all about the dance floor and dinner table; I also love to model, and I love nail art. It is a creative outlet for me, and I find it fascinating to express different aspects of myself through photography, fashion, and nail art.

As an advocate for transgender rights, I' am committed to making the world a more inclusive place. This journey has taught me resilience and prizing authenticity.

If you are someone who appreciates positivity, values adventure and believes in embracing life's' beauty', I'd love to hear from you. Let's create some amazing memories together!

Yours truly!
Tamara Rivera

In the vast realm of online dating and occasional encounters with troublesome individuals, I find solace in my extensive circle of friends and followers on Facebook, Instagram, and TikTok. However, amidst this digital landscape, I have encountered a distressing dating dilemma.

To protect myself, I have resorted to blocking those who request my WhatsApp tag, particularly those who claim to be generous and express a desire to send me money. Yet, despite my cautious nature, I fell victim to a scam that forced me to close my account.

The internet has undoubtedly brought visibility to transgender individuals, but it has also exposed them to vulnerability. Many online individuals engage in malicious acts, targeting unsuspecting victims through social media and connected apps.

It is disheartening to realize that no one truly has your financial success in mind. Beware of those who feign care, for they are merely pretenders. There are cookie-cutter responses specifically crafted to lure women and transgender individuals with false intentions.

As time passed, I blocked countless individuals who partook in such deceitful practices. If you examine the subtext carefully, you will discern the language used to captivate your interest.

The WE Group for Women

For two years, I served as the bilingual administrator of a women's support group on Facebook. During this time, I met the founder of the group, forming a close friendship with them. With my ability to speak both English and Spanish, I was able to connect with women from different linguistic backgrounds.

My main responsibility was to create engaging and positive content in a bilingual format, which I did by posting at least twice a day. Additionally, I actively took part in group chat sessions, where women appreciated my positive outlook and encouraging content. Through this experience, I had the chance to meet women from all over the US on a near-daily basis.

It was truly an interesting journey, as I not only shared my knowledge and experiences with these women but also learned a great deal from them. Some even trusted me enough to confide personal problems that they wouldn't have shared with anyone else. I am grateful that these women treated me with respect, regardless of my transgender identity. They accepted me as a genetic woman, and throughout the active period of the group, many of these women happily engaged with me.

The primary administrator of the group closed it due to health reasons, resulting in everyone losing access. However, this closure did not mark the end of my connection with some of the women I inspired. Some of them stayed in contact with me, remaining my friends and allies to this day.

The women are aware of my transgender identity, but it has never posed a problem in our friendship. When you lead by example and consistently share uplifting messages, people appreciate and continue to follow and engage with you. We all need someone to uplift us at times, and I know this well. If I ever post something that conveys sadness, pain, or sickness, they respond with encouraging and positive thoughts.

FAB OVER 40

A vote for Change for Tamara Rivera!

Hello everyone,

I am a transgender woman breaking the barriers and boundaries others say I couldn't, and 'competing where competition is fierce, I am the first transgender woman competing in the FabOver40 contest to receive a 2-page spread in NewBeauty magazine, $40,000 cash, and a spa-cation! to benefit the National Breast Cancer Foundation INC.

My journey as a transgender woman has taught me prizing embracing and standing up for the rights of all individuals. Now, I'm looking for your support.

By voting for me, you're also supporting my personal growth and advocating for inclusivity, diversity, and the limitless potential that exists within each of us.

Let us break barriers, shatter stereotypes, and prove that Fab Over 40 is not just a contest; it is a movement for change. Join me in making a difference.

Support Tamara Rivera's campaign and let's create a more inclusive world.

Thank you for your support! #FabOver40 #InclusivityMatters #VoteForChange Vote here: https://votefab40.com/2023/Tamara-rivera

The failures of Online Dating

Please exercise caution and avoid the pitfalls and failures of online dating based on my personal experience.

You can never be certain who you're talking to. In my quest for a potential partner through online dating, I have experimented with various apps and social media platforms frequently, but unfortunately, I had no luck finding one that truly works, regardless of whether I invest financially.

The level of deception and danger associated with these apps is significantly higher, and regrettably, Facebook does not contribute to improving their safety or reliability.

Instead of encountering pleasant interactions or memorable dates, what I experienced were instances of appalling male behavior, and sometimes, even situations that posed a significant risk to my safety.

Based on my observations, it has become clear that most men online, are primarily focused on creating an illusion of love in order to satisfy their own desires. They skillfully employ eloquent language that can make you feel exceptionally special. However, much like a skilled angler, when they sense you are falling for their charm, they suddenly present you with outrageous demands. It appears they have already cast their fishing line and are now eagerly preparing to reel you in.

Over time, it has become a widespread practice for these men to establish a designated virtual space where they gather to discuss and agree upon standardized responses, all to captivate your interest.

Frequently, I have come across situations were men approach women with requests for financial help, specifically to get an Apple card. Supposedly, this request is made to ensure uninterrupted communication with you.

To gain your trust, they often masquerade as high-ranking military officers stationed in the United States. Some even go to the extent of pretending to possess immense wealth, flaunting luxurious mansions and expensive cars, or claiming to work on offshore oil rigs.

However, one cannot help but question the authenticity of their claimed affluence. The glimmer of uncertainty dances in the air as they ask you to foot the bill for a calling card, their voice tinged with a hint of desperation.

Thoughts swirl like a whirlwind as you ponder why someone with such wealth would suddenly claim that their phone broke, their plea for help echoing in your mind.

On one occasion, a man with a charming smile approached, his persuasive voice carrying a melody that seemed almost too perfect. He asked me to buy him an iPhone on my account, promising to wire the money to my bank account. Yet, a red flag unfurled in the depths of my consciousness.

The sound of his words, like a siren's call, clashed with the uncertainty in his eyes, creating a dissonance that sent shivers down my spine.

Another red flag emerges, a warning sign amidst the digital landscape. It begins innocently enough, with individuals reaching out through dating apps or social media platforms. But then, a private message arrives, urging you to switch to secretive chat apps like Google Chat, WhatsApp, or Snapchat.

The air thickens with suspicion as you realize these platforms, where they spend their time searching for potential victims, are like dark alleys filled with deception and manipulation.

In my case, a man appeared on a dating app for transgender women, claiming to be a philanthropist. His words, filled with intense emotions, reverberated in my ears like a symphony of promises.

He openly declared his desire to provide financial support my transition surgery, his unwavering love for me echoing through the digital realm. Yet, amidst the chorus of his declarations, a whisper of doubt lingers, questioning the authenticity of his intentions.

As our conversation unfolded, the sound of his voice filled the air, calmly mentioning the tragic loss of his spouse. The words carried a certain familiarity that struck me deeply, like a well-rehearsed script. It felt like a manipulative tactic I had witnessed before, designed to captivate the attention of unsuspecting women, evoking sympathy and leading them to fall in love blindly.

Initially, my interest was piqued, but it didn't take long for me to notice a recurring pattern in his storytelling, and spoke of being in Dubai, engrossed in a lucrative investment deal, while simultaneously mentioning his sick uncle in California who urgently needed medication.

A sense of regret filled his voice as he explained his inability to provide financial help, claiming his resources were fully invested and inaccessible.

It was then that I realized his hidden agenda, subtly asking me to cover the costs of his uncle's treatment. Without hesitation, I swiftly responded, firmly asserting my inability to help. The weight of his uncle's potential demise did not rest on my shoulders.

This encounter reminded me of a similar incident in the past, when another man reached out to me on Facebook shortly after becoming friends. He wasted no time in requesting that we switch to Google chat for further communication, a request to which I reluctantly agreed.

Over the course of a few conversations, I developed feelings for him. However, everything changed when I woke up one day to find his final message, which contained a shocking revelation.

He sent a message with a disturbing plan to manipulate and exploit women. He admitted to being a sexual predator who wanted to sell them as sex slaves. Also, he mentioned he didn't think I deserved his actions and gave me the option to block him. The experience of falling into a dangerous situation has had a profound impact on me, leading me to lose trust in men online.

Moving forward, whenever a man sends me a request to be friends, I swiftly block his access without no explanation, ensuring that he doesn't perceive me as an easy target. The countless instances of men attempting to deceive and take advantage of me on social media have left me skeptical of trusting both men and women on these platforms.

By opting for local, secure social gatherings, you can easily differentiate between authentic individuals and those who may pretend to be someone they are not. The rise of social media has had a significant effect on the visibility of trans people, both positively and negatively.

While it has allowed them to be more visible online, it has also made them more susceptible to predators who prey on vulnerable individuals. I urge you to be cautious whenever you interact with anyone online and not to risk your life becoming another statistic of the late-night news, another transgender woman tragically losing her life to crime.

"Don't wake a sleeping lion, unless you want to be lunch."

– Tamara Rivera

COX ENTERPRISES

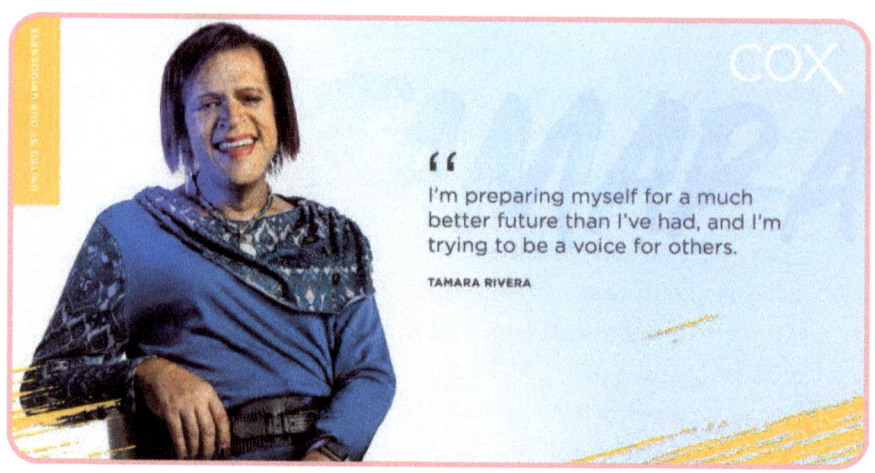

Recognitions

"I was always scared of what would happen if I came out as transgender woman. Would I lose my job? What about my family?"

We continue to celebrate National Coming Out Week and the stories of LGBTQIA+ individuals and allies. Below, Tamara Rivera of Cox shares her story.

"I came out at 59, and the choice was clear, since I was already wearing women's clothes beneath my male outer shell.

I was not going to continue dressing up behind closed doors. "I was always scared of what would happen if I came out as transgender.

Would I lose my job?

What about my family?

I walked the halls of the office many times looking at women and how beautiful they looked in the clothes and colors they wore and imagining myself dressed as they dressed. But I always had that question in my head that made me so afraid of taking the step to come out. What will happen if I lose my job?

Back in 2013, I was fortunate enough to have a chance to fully express myself during the office's Halloween dress-up contest. I went all out by dressing up in women's attire from head to toe, complete with a pair of 4½-inch high heels and a stylish wig.

Little did anyone know that was the true measure of who I am inside. Despite my pride in wearing those clothes that day, a sense of sadness lingered within me, uncertain if I would ever have the opportunity again. As I walked out of the office, clutching the prize for the dress-up contest, I couldn't help but feel that it didn't truly represent who I wanted to be known for. What I truly desired was recognition for who I am at my core - the person I yearned to come out as.

As I reflect on my decision to confide in my supervisor as a transgender individual, I chose this company because of its reputation as an LGBTQ+ friendly organization. It was crucial for me to feel confident that my employer would be there to support me throughout this journey. This company has consistently provided me with support in various ways. However, the moment holds utmost significance for me.

I had a Teams meeting about a week after coming out, in which my supervisor introduced me as Tamara Rivera. That day there was some confusion, as some people were asking,

"Who is Tamara?" I saw the first message in the chatroom. Someone privately informed me that my name was misspelled. Everyone congratulated me for my courage when my coming out journey was announced.

"National Coming Out Day is very important. Socially, we have grown so much, but politically there are a lot of barriers against the LGBTQ+ community based on standards, religious and social stigma, beliefs and hate. Just because we are different.

Throughout my upbringing, and even in the present day, I've noticed that a significant number of individuals hold a negative perception of transgender people. Interestingly, while society is more accepting of gays and lesbians, there remains a pressing need for greater education and understanding when it comes to the transgender community.

As individuals with diverse talents and backgrounds, we collectively bring a wealth of skills and experiences to the workforce, making us invaluable assets for any business aiming for success. Personally, I am striving for a brighter future, one that surpasses my experiences. I am determined to use my voice to advocate for others, recognizing the newfound strength and influence it grants me.

#NationalComingOutDay #pride #lifeatcox

Transgender Advocacy

Before I made my public declaration, I already had an intense connection to the LGBTQIA+ community. There were moments when I would silently cry as I witnessed the injustice faced by those who identified themselves outside the conventional binary definitions of male and female.

These instances were often highlighted in the news, especially the unjust treatment of transgender women. It pained me to see them being forced to use the men's bathroom instead of the gender-specific facilities they deserved. Even worse, some transgender women were victims of violence, robbed, or even murdered simply for being true to themselves.

The unjustifiable treatment we witness is completely unacceptable. Despite this, we still observe politicians pushing their agenda and using their power to create legislation that further humiliates and punishes individuals for being different. For example, individuals may employ phrases such as "men in women's clothing" to rationalize the mistreatment of girls in restrooms. It is crucial to underscore that this behavior is unacceptable. There is no need for men to disguise themselves as women to enter a restroom and perpetrate acts of abuse, rape, or murder against unsuspecting victims. It is important to remember, transgender individuals are compassionate, affectionate, and considerate human beings who warrant respect and the opportunity to express their gender identity with honor.

A small group misrepresents gender, causing chaos and exploiting others. However, before criminalizing an entire community, it is important to conduct a careful study to understand their desire for love and respect. In line with this, since September 2021, my primary focus has been writing letters to support the transgender community.

I am working diligently to raise awareness and establish laws that protect us. It is unfortunate that religious groups and politicians have largely mistreated and abused our community. I remain committed to my cause. Below, you will find a copy of the letters I sent to the White House and congressional leaders in my state. I will continue to do everything in my power to advocate for the transgender community.

I have used slogans at the end of each chapter. Some of them are my own inspiration, while others represent the voices of others. When we reflect on the powerful voices that have made an impact in society, there are many examples throughout history. However, my personal favorite is the quote below, which has served as my inspiration for creating letters of advocacy.

"The voice of one is more powerful than the force of a thousand souls."

— *Tamara Rivera*

From the desk of Tamara Rivera
To the Attention of: The White House
Subject: Advocating for Gender Choices on Legal Documents

Dear President: Joseph R. Biden, Jr.

I hope this letter finds you in good health and high spirits. I am writing to bring to your attention a subject close at heart to an important matter that affects a significant portion of our population. I strongly advocate for implementing laws across all states to allow individuals to choose a gender other than male or female on legal documents in the USA.

In recent years, our society has witnessed a remarkable growth in awareness and understanding of gender diversity as well as new laws affecting transgender rights across the country. It is now widely recognized that gender identity exists on a spectrum and that not everyone identifies strictly as male or female. This understanding has led to greater recognition of the rights and dignity of individuals who identify as non-binary, genderqueer, or other gender identities beyond the binary.

However, despite the progress made, there still exists a significant gap in legal recognition for these individuals such as me. Many states within our great nation require individuals to identify as either male or female on official documents such as driver's licenses, passports, and birth certificates. This binary approach cannot acknowledge and respect the lived experiences and identities of those who identify outside of the male-female construct.

The absence of legal recognition for individuals who identify as non-binary or have other gender identities can lead to many challenges and hardships. It hampers our ability to access essential services, such as healthcare, education, and employment, with dignity and without discrimination. It also creates unnecessary confusion and distress when these individuals are forced to choose a gender that does not align with their gender identity.

By implementing laws that allow individuals to choose a gender other than male or female on legal documents, we can take a significant step forward in promoting inclusivity, respect, and equal treatment for all Americans.

Such legislation would not only reflect the evolving understanding of gender identity but also align with the principles of fairness, individual autonomy, and human rights that our nation upholds.

Several jurisdictions, both within our country and around the world, have already embraced these progressive measures. They have successfully implemented gender-neutral or non-binary gender options on official documents, providing individuals with the freedom to express their gender identity authentically. We learn from their experiences and follow suit, ensuring that the United States remains at the forefront of progress in safeguarding the rights and well-being of all its citizens.

As the leader of our nation, your support and commitment to this cause would send a powerful message of inclusivity, equality, and respect for diversity. By championing the implementation of laws that allow individuals to choose a gender other than male or female on all legal documents, you would help to shape a future where everyone's gender identity is acknowledged, respected, and honored.

Thank you for considering my plea and for your tireless dedication to creating a more inclusive and fair society. I remain hopeful that, under your leadership, our nation will take this important step toward recognizing and embracing the gender identities of all its citizens, by this, I am raising my voice for all in the transgender community.

With the deepest respect,
Sincerely yours
Tamara Rivera
Advocating In Support of Transgender Rights.

THE WHITE HOUSE
WASHINGTON

August 2, 2023

Dear Ms. Rivera,

Despite the progress they have achieved in recent decades, transgender Americans continue to face discrimination and violence. A wave of hateful bills has been advanced across the country to strip transgender Americans of their rights, ban transgender children from playing sports, and outlaw the discussion of LGBTQI+ people in schools. These attacks are un-American, are hurting transgender youth, and are putting loving families at risk of harassment and discrimination. I will always have the backs of transgender Americans so they can enjoy the freedom and equality promised to all Americans. After issuing the first-ever National Strategy on Gender Equity and Equality, I was proud to ensure that transgender Americans can reflect their accurate gender identity on federal identification documents, restore the right for transgender Americans to serve openly in our military, and bolster services for transgender veterans. I am also strengthening federal non-discrimination protections, addressing anti-transgender violence, and working to guarantee that transgender Americans can access the health care they need. I won't stop there. I will continue to call on Congress to pass the Equality Act so LGBTQI+ individuals cannot be denied a home, a job, an education, and more because of who they are or whom they love. Transgender people are some of the bravest Americans I know, and our Nation is stronger and more vibrant because of them. Together, we will continue to strive for a world free from discrimination and violence against the transgender community.

Sincerely,

Joe Biden

RAPHAEL WARNOCK
GEORGIA

United States Senate
WASHINGTON, DC 20510-1012

Dear Tamara,

Thank you for contacting me to share your support for protecting transgender youth.

Our youth are the next generation's leaders, and I believe it is our responsibility to help brighten their futures and expand their opportunities. As a man of faith who proudly supports the LGBTQ+ community, I believe deeply in the sacred worth of all people. I will always fight to protect civil rights, and I am committed to ensuring that everyone has equal access to opportunity. Our country progresses each time we right the injustices of our past.

That is why I proudly co-sponsored and voted to pass the Respect for Marriage Act, which protects marriage equality for all. And on December 13, 2022, President Biden signed this vital legislation into law. I am also a proud co-sponsor of S. 5, the Equality Act, which would prohibit discrimination on the basis of sexual orientation or gender identity in employment, housing, and public accommodations.

As you may know, Georgia Drivers Licenses are handled by the Georgia Department of Motor Vehicles and fall under the jurisdiction of the state. Therefore, I encourage you to reach out to your local representatives to share your concerns. You may find your state legislator here: https://www.legis.ga.gov/find-my-legislator.

Should legislation on this issue come to U.S. Congress, please know that I will keep your views in mind. In the meantime, know that I will continue working with my colleagues in the U.S. Senate to protect the rights of all Georgians.

Thank you again for contacting me. Please do not hesitate to do so again in the future if I may be of help to you or your family.

Sincerely,

Reverend Raphael Warnock
United States Senator

ROCK SPRINGS
www.RockSprings.biz info@RockSprings.us

To Whom It May Concern,

August 14, 2023

I am writing this letter on behalf of my client, Tamara Rivera (DOB: 05/30/1962) and with her permission. She seeks to move forward with laser hair removal and gender-affirming surgery (man to woman).

Tamara Rivera is a 61-year-old individual. She reports that she is currently employed fulltime as an Online Technical Support Agent and lives in a house that she rents with two roommates.

She also reports having a good social support system: a trans-affirming Church that she attends weekly for services, her two children, her ex-wife whom she describes as her "best friend," and her social media following of over 1500 individuals that is a source of "positivity" and "encouragement."

I first met Tamara Rivera in April 2021. She was initially referred to Rock Springs by her physician, Dr. Douglas Gurley, for support in coming-out as a woman and socially transitioning.

After meeting with my colleague, David Harris (Executive Director), for two intake sessions, she was referred to me for therapy. However, Tamara and I met for only one session although I stayed in communication through the end of that month (April 2021) when it became clear that financial support for therapy was very limited.

She reported that she would reach out to her employer for low-fee resources.

Since then, Tamara reports that she has built connections in the LGBT community and taken steps in transitioning, such as dressing in women's clothing and wearing make-up.

In June 2023, Tamara reached out to my organization Rock Springs Positive Coaching, Caring, and Counseling, INC for the purpose of obtaining this letter of endorsement.

We have met weekly for a total of four sessions. In addition to these sessions, Tamara completed a battery of screenings (please see attached third page). The results from the screenings do not raise any serious reservations that would negatively impact the outcome of gender-affirming medical treatments.

Tamara reports a long-standing history of gender dysphoria related to her assignment as male at birth. She reported that she had internal challenges with accepting herself and the body she was born with beginning at the age of five years old. She reports that she has been medically transitioning since early 2021 under the care of Duane Moody, FNP-C and has been socially transitioned since 1983. She meets the criteria for Gender Dysphoria (F64.0).

She clearly articulates her reasons for desiring surgery, the risks, and benefits, the implications of this procedure, and the impact it would have on her gender presentation and life. She reports that she has done the necessary research and built up a stable support system to aid in her recovery.

She seems to demonstrate sufficient insight, judgment, and decision-making capacity necessary for consent. She reports that she has resources and a positive support system. She meets the WPATH SOCS criteria, which is why I am providing this letter of support for her to continue her exploration of gender-affirming surgery.

As Tamara continues to move forward in the transition process, it is my recommendation (and hope) that she will continue with therapy to support her recovery, including navigating the mental, social, and emotional aspects following the surgery.

I am a fully licensed marriage and family therapist (LMFT) and have been providing therapy since 2018 to LGBT individuals and others.

Natalia Gourlay-Fernandez, LMFT
Licensed Marriage and Family Therapist
License #MFTOO 1899
Natalia.Gourlay-Fernandez@RockSprings.us

Date 3/27/2023
Name: Tamara Rivera
Pronoun: She/Her
Date established care with referring provider 1/26/2021
Procedure sought: Bottom Surgery
Date began living full time in identified gender: 2021
Taking hormones (Y/N): Yes
Date hormones started: 5/21
City, state of primary residence: Dallas, GA
Stable: permanent housing (Y/N): Yes

To Whom It May Concern:

Tamara is a patient under my care. Tamara has the gender identity of a female which is well established and stable. By my independent evaluation, I have diagnosed her with Gender Dysphoria (ICD-10 F64.1F64.9) She reports symptoms of anxiety and depression, which she feels are exacerbated by this Dysphoria. She relates much of her Gender Dysphoria to her male genitalia. Tamara has expressed a persistent desire for bottom surgery. She has sufficient social support to move through the surgical process. I believe Tamara would benefit greatly both medically and psychologically from bottom surgery. This bottom surgery has been defined as medically necessary by the World Professional Association for Transgender Health.

Additionally, Tamara is medically stable for surgery. Her/his medical history is significant for hypertension and elevated cholesterol. Her BMI is 23.18 (required<35 for surgery). She does not smoke cigarettes or drink excessive alcohol and is not at risk of or an active user f illicit drugs or drugs of abuse.

Tamara has met the WPATH SOCv7 criteria for surgery. I feel she has the capacity to provide informed consent for bottom surgery, and she is ready, appropriate and medically clear for this bottom surgery. I hereby recommend and refer Tamara for this surgery. Please feel free to contact me with any questions or concerns.

Sincerely,

Duane Moody, FNP-C

659 Auburn Avenue NE Suite 156 Atlanta, GA 30312 PHONE 404 888 0228
FAX 404 888 0552
www.tdauglasgurleymd.com

Jamie M. Joseph, Ph.D.
Licensed Psychologist
Cognitive Behavior Therapy & Consultation

www.jamiemjosephphd.com
jamiemjoseph@hushmail.com
Phone: (954) 684-6336

Dear Dr. Whitehead,

Thank you for the courtesy of referring your patient, Tamara Rivera (DOB = 5-30-62) for a 'Presurgical Psychological Consultation' for her requested 'Minimal Depth Vaginoplasty' surgery. As you know, I am a Licensed Psychologist* with a specialization in gender diversity concerns and as a professional member of the World Professional Association for Transgender Health (WPATH), I follow their standards of care for my profession. I appreciate the opportunity to collaborate and coordinate multidisciplinary and personalized care with Tamara and you.

I met with Tamara for two video telehealth sessions (11-14-23 & 1-12-24 – for approximately an hour and 15 minutes total). Tamara participated from her home in Powder Springs, Georgia and she was able to arrange for privacy, confidentiality, and comfort to speak freely in that setting. In advance of the session, Informed Consent and HIPAA regulations were provided, all via encrypted email. It is noteworthy that all the information discussed here is based on Tamara's self-report. A summary of relevant details from the sessions and a telephone consultation you and I had about Tamara are highlighted in this letter.

Tamara, age 61, was assigned male at birth and she identifies as a transgender woman. She has been waiting a long time for her bottom surgical feminization. Tamara presented in both consultation sessions as sweet, warm, and enthusiastic. She was immediately likable and friendly. Working rapport was established easily and maintained throughout both meetings.

Tamara presented with logical thoughts and was focused to person, time, and place. She maintained appropriate eye contact. She exhibited positive mood and hopefulness for the post-surgical recovery outcome physically and psychologically.

Tamara was cooperative with all required of her to participate in this consultation without hesitation. Her positive energy made working with her very pleasant.

Cognitive Behavior Therapy & Consultation
2 Tamara is employed full time by 'My employer' as a 'Technical Client Service Representative.' The company has been supportive of her gender transition without any difficulty or discrimination. She works remotely. She is satisfied with her work, but it can be stressful, and customers can be demanding.

She anticipates she will be able to take Family Medical Leave to undergo and recover from her gender confirmation surgery.

Tamara began living full-time as a transgender woman in 2021, transitioning socially and medically (hormones). Prior, she had been living with her (now) ex-wife and their children, who are adults in their twenties (still living in the family home). Given 'some tension' in the house once she transitioned, she moved out for two years. However, for economic reasons she moved back in with them, as supporting two homes financially was not possible.

Presently she reports an amicable relationship with her ex-wife and adult children and her housing situation is stable and consistent.

Tamara has "always dreamed of" having a vagina since she was a child. Gender dysphoria with her male gender assigned at birth date back to early childhood. Prior to medical and socially transitioning she wore feminine clothing at times in the privacy in her home. For this reason, she thinks her ex-wife and children were 'not surprised' when she tells them she was socially and medically transitioning full time.

She wishes she had transitioned at a younger age, but "life got in the way and times were different." Psychologically Tamara has had heightened challenges with anxiety and depression in the past several years relating to her gender identity, life changes and occupational stressors.

She took a medical leave from her job to "work it out to the best of my ability. "She had sessions with "five to six therapists over the past three years," most of whom were from the employee help program offered through her job.

Presently she is emotionally stable. She has never had any suicidal or homicidal ideation. She reported no history of psychotic episodes or encounters with the law.

Tamara is in "the best shape of" her life. She lost 47 lbs. two years ago by exercising 45 minutes daily at 6:00 AM, changing her mindset and eating a low salt, low sugar, low-fat diet.

She does not use or abuse legal or illegal drugs; she does not smoke or vape at all. She rarely drinks alcohol.

Regarding social support and coping with challenge, Tamara is very involved at her church and finds comfort, purpose and peace in religion and spirituality. She is socially well connected at a church that is gender affirmative, and she has a meaningful connection with the pastor and fellow congregants. She also has a supportive online social media network, and she advocates for transgender equality.

Tamara enjoys housing stability and lives with her ex-wife and adult children with cordial relationships and interactions. She has her own bedroom in the home and is comfortable with the arrangement. When we met the first time in December, she was in the process of publishing a book she wrote about growing up as a transgender person.

Just after our second meeting she informed me her book will be on sale soon, available through Doris Penn Publishing and media sales outlets. Writing is an excellent

3 emotionally cathartic for Tamara and has served as a vehicle processing challenging, and difficult emotions.

Tamara understands that a Minimal Depth Vaginoplasty is medically appropriate for her after two consultations with Dr. Whitehead and she was able to discuss why this is the case with me. At our initial meeting, Tamara (11-14-23), she was not clear on how the surgery would impact her sexual functioning or what the specific aftercare needs would be.

Also, she had not yet planned for a companion to accompany her to surgery and stay in Miami for the initial recovery and in Georgia if needed. I assisted Tamara in formulating questions to ask / discuss with Dr. Whitehead about the surgery.

Additionally, she agreed to speak with her pastor about seeking help from person who can accompany her to Miami for the surgery and assist with aftercare for the duration of her stay and until she is able to care for herself. I advised Tamara once she had a second Medical Presurgical Consultation with Dr. Whitehead, and investigated securing aftercare help, we'd re-meet to review these details.

Additionally, Dr. Whitehead, you and I discussed Tamara's need for clarity on surgical results and recovery necessities.

Tamara and I met a second time on 1-12-24. She was able to competently discuss the risks and benefits of the Minimal Depth Vaginoplasty surgery at that meeting. Dr. Whitehead, you had also notified me of the meeting and reported she understood the discussion and asked relevant questions. Additionally, Tamara reported she spoke with a close friend who agreed to assist her with aftercare in Miami and back home in Georgia as needed.

In both Presurgical Psychological Consultation sessions, Tamara and I discussed the fact that bottom surgery is an irreversible medical intervention and that there will be pain and discomfort associated with the procedure. She understands there will be extensive aftercare procedures to follow for both health and healing purposes. Importantly, I processed with Tamara it is impossible to know in advance if she will experience regret for choosing to have her gender confirmation surgery in the future. She expressed understanding of this possibility, however doubted she would have regret given the fact she has dreamed about having feminine genitalia instead of male since childhood.

Tamara thoughtfully expressed she anticipates she will benefit psychologically from her gender confirmation surgery as it is commensurate with her long-standing embodiment of her female gender identity.

Tamara presented as an excellent candidate for gender confirmation surgery (Minimal Depth Vaginoplasty) as a medical intervention for diagnosed Gender Dysphoria in Adolescents and Adults (F64.1). I did not identify psychological barriers to surgical transition, and symptoms of anxiety and / or depression are under control as of the date of this letter.

Tamara has arranged for help for aftercare and has a supportive community for recovery. Her housing is stable, and she lives with an accepting family in addition to being employed for years. Tamara is highly motivated to achieve her longstanding vision of her body with external genital anatomy that matches her gender identity. It is my professional opinion she is psychologically ready to move forward with surgery.

4 If you have any questions or would like to discuss Tamara's case history further, please call me at (954) 684-6336 and I'd be happy to coordinate care with you.

Respectfully,
Jamie M. Joseph, Ph.D.
Jamie M. Joseph, Ph.D.
Licensed Psychologist*
(electronically signed)10-23-23.
CC: Tamara Rivera

*Licensed Psychologist in New York & Florida. Dr. Joseph has also obtained an Authority to Practice Interjurisdictional Telepsychology (APIT) from the PSYPACT Commission (through the state of Florida).

Dear Reader,

Thank you for taking the time to walk with me through the pages of *Becoming Tamara*. Your willingness to share in my journey means more to me than words can express. This book represents not just my story but the universal struggle to embrace authenticity and live boldly as our truest selves.

As you've read, my path has been marked by trials, triumphs, doubt, and discovery. It was a journey I walked not only for myself but for anyone who has ever felt unseen, unheard, or uncertain about their place in the world. My hope is that through my story, you've found a spark of inspiration, whether it is the courage to take your next step or the strength to uplift someone else on their journey.

Remember, each of us holds the power to live authentically and unapologetically. Your truth is beautiful, and your voice matters. I am honored that *Becoming Tamara* could be part of your story, and I hope it leaves you feeling empowered and encouraged.

Thank you for allowing me to share my heart with you. Together, we can create a world where authenticity is celebrated, and everyone feels free to live their truth.

With gratitude and hope,
Tamara Rivera

About the Author

Tamara Rivera is a dynamic author who skillfully uses her powerful storytelling to advocate for transgender rights and brings visibility to underrepresented voices. In her work, she seamlessly combines personal experiences with universal themes of resilience, courage, and self-discovery, creating a compelling narrative that invites readers to join her on a journey marked by both struggle and triumph. Through her memoir, Becoming Tamara, she offers a raw and honest portrayal of her own transformation, shedding light on the complexities of embracing one's true self.

As a digital creator with a large, engaged following, Tamara extends her influence beyond the written page. She fosters community and inspires positivity through her engaging online presence. Her passion for fashion, beauty, and creativity flows into her work. This reflects a vibrant individuality that resonates deeply with readers and followers alike. Tamara's work is a testament to her resilience and commitment to authenticity and inclusivity. It is a constant reminder of her unyielding pursuit of a world where everyone feels empowered to be themselves.

www.ingramcontent.com/pod-product-compliance
Lightning Source LLC
LaVergne TN
LVHW061531070526
838199LV00010B/452